Transport
AIR TRANSPORT

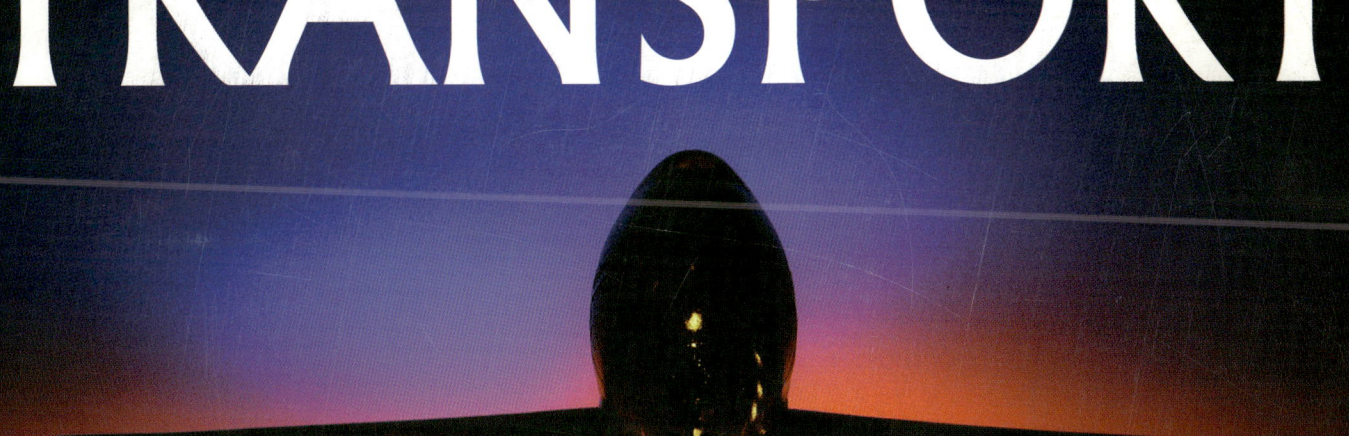

Edited by: Pallabi B. Tomar
Managing editor: Tapasi De
Designed by: Vijesh Chahal, Anil Kumar and Rohit Kumar
Illustrated by: Suman S. Roy, Tanoy Choudhury
Colouring done by: Vinay Kumar, Sonu, Kiran Kumari & Pradeep Kumar

CONTENTS

Introduction 3

History of air transport 4

Types of air transport 7

Vehicles of air transport 9

Airport 12

Air traffic control (ATC) 14

Advantages of air transport 15

Disadvantages of air transport 18

Role in economic development 19

Limitations of air transport services 22

Famous aircraft manufacturers 24

Largest air transport crafts 26

Test Your Memory 31

Index 32

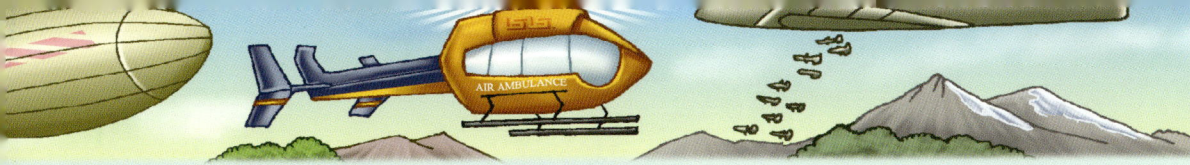

Introduction

Transport of men, mail and materials through a vehicle in the air from one place to another is referred to as air transport. The vehicle in case of air transport is termed as aircraft. Aircraft is a vehicle operating primarily in the Earth's atmosphere but at appreciable distances above the ground.

The growth of air transport has modified the travel habits of millions of people and has influenced socio-political and economic life of the people in many countries. These effects have been made possible not only by the rapid technological development of the aircraft, but also by the introduction of uniform navigational and communication facilities throughout the world. The progressive evolution of international air agreements, regulation, rules of flight, conduct and regulatory agencies together provide a worldwide code of civil aircraft operation.

Air transport is very fast and reaches long distances in a very short time. It has even the advantage of linking remote as well as isolated areas without adequate and proper means of transport and across dense forests, deserts, oceans and mountain barriers. All the aeroplanes follow chartered routes marked by modern mechanical devices such as radio beams and beacons. They are controlled by control towers that control the location, altitude and speed of planes at all times.

Air transport has become an essential economic and social conduit throughout the world. Beyond the benefits of fast and inexpensive transcontinental travel, air transport has also become a vital form of shipping for high value items that need to come to market quickly, such as agricultural products subject to spoilage. Modern jet aircrafts are capable of crossing vast distances at high speeds.

Astonishing fact

During the earliest years of airmail flights, pilots were guided through the darkness by bonfires set along air routes!

AIR TRANSPORT

History of air transport

Air transportation in our present scenario plays a very important role. Airlines do provide their service by allowing people to go to any location they desire. Man was first assured that they could enjoy flying through use of kites.

The Europeans made use of gliders in the ninth century. In the Renaissance period, Leonardo da Vinci had designed over hundred sketching of certain ideas to make these flying objects. The Montgolfier brothers were the first ones to introduce the hot air balloons in 1783 in Paris.

The initial introduction of flying objects was seen in China, where kites and balloons and kites that used hot-air were extensively used. However, the inaugural official flight happened in 1903 at North Carolina. The aeroplane was invented by none other than the Wright Brothers. Soon enough sea planes entered the scene as well. It was invented by French designer and engineer, named Henri Fabre in 1910. The first helicopter was practically flown by Focke Achgelis in 1936. After that, air transportation only got better and smoother. The golden period in air transportation was in between 1918 and 1940.These years saw some of the remarkable achievements when it came to inventing military aircrafts.

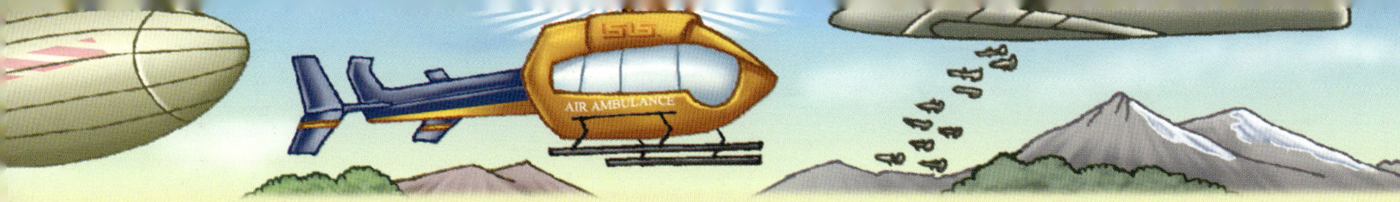

History of air transport

Jet engines, barnstormers, fighter escorts and jet planes just brightened the scene. The maximum use of aircrafts, helicopters and jet planes were done during World War I and World War II. The inauguration of commercial airplanes was seen during the Cold War. The airliner Tupolev Tu-104 operated consistently by providing number of services to citizens in 1956 in former U.S.S.R. However, owing to the overture of Boeing 707, air travel got a new meaning. Travelling became bit more relaxed, sophisticated, met luxurious demand of customers and was considered safe.

It is difficult to imagine not being able to catch a flight to travel around the world these days, but this technology has not been around for that long. The first ever controlled heavier-than-air controlled flight occurred within Connecticut by Gustave Whitehead in 1901. This predated the famous Wright Brothers flight by a whole two years. Whitehead's engine powered plane with glider-like wings flew over 800 m at an altitude of 15 m.

Since then, replicas of Whitehead's plane have been flown successfully, his flight becoming the first real milestone in heavier-than-air powered flight in the 19th century. The highly publicized flights of the Wright Brothers however are far more well-known, with the flights they organised in Carolina in December, 1903. These were regarded by the Federation Aeronautique Internationale (FAI) as the first sustained and controlled heavier-than-air power flight.

To communicate with passengers in the 1930s, cabin crew often had to resort to speaking through small megaphones to be heard above the din of the engines and the wind.

AIR TRANSPORT

Air transportation was very popular in the first decade of the 20th century with many different inventors making claims of short flights. Many of these were verified and others were not. Lyman Gilmore claimed to have flown a plane successfully in 1902 but there were no witnesses to back this up. A farmer in New Zealand claimed to have created a monoplane that flew in March 1903. The Wright Brothers continued to conduct flights in Ohio during the years 1904 and 1905, inviting their family and friends to witness. Due to a failed attempt that occurred in 1904, members of the media did not attend and witness the later flights.

The history of the powered flight in air transportation created a major boost within the First World War (1914-1918), when manned planes were used by allies and central powers. Planes were used for the air transportation of aid and directly created air attacks. In the beginning, people found it bizarre to use the plane as a weapon but it soon became adopted.

Today air transportation is very important for many different reasons, but is still prominent in warfare and has changed the essence of war and travel across the world. Engineering specialists today are required to offer many services to aviation, in particular, security. Much planning and work is needed for the building of airports and plane terminals. Also much study is necessary to check the environmental impacts air transportation has created. Much planning and work is needed for the building of airports and plane terminals. Also much study is necessary to check the environmental impacts air transportation has created.

Astonishing fact

Earl Ovington performed the first airmail delivery during a demonstration flight in 1911 by simply dropping a bag of mail overboard, which was picked up by a postmaster.

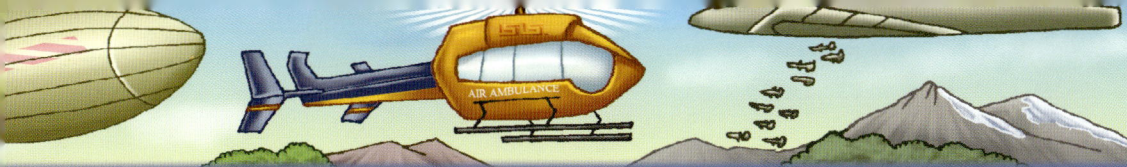

Types of air transport

Aviation can be broadly divided into three areas:

- Commercial Aviation
- General Aviation
- Military Aviation

Commercial Aviation

Commercial aviation or commercial air transport is offered by airlines such as American Airlines, Royal Brunei, British Airways, Lufthansa, and Singapore Airlines, etc., while airlines such as Cargolux and Delta Airlines operate passenger and cargo flights.

This type of aviation started after World War I using mostly ex-military aircraft for the purpose of transporting people and goods for profit. A profitable cargo was air mail, which was the means by which governments subsidized air travel. In October 1929 the Graf Zeppelin, a large German passenger-carrying airship inaugurated the first commercial transatlantic service. In May 6, 1937, the airship Hindenburg burned and marked the end of the airship era. Before that airships or dirigible were a major mode of long-distance air travel.

After World War II the introduction of jetliners allowed large numbers of people to be quickly transported.

Astonishing fact

Since its introduction in 1969, the entire fleet of Boeing 747s has logged enough miles to make more than 70,000 trips to the moon and back.

AIR TRANSPORT

General Aviation

General aviation is a term comprising all of aviation other than military and scheduled air transport (airlines). It includes privately owned aircraft, charter services, business owned aircraft, such as 'bizjets,' and many more types of working aircraft that are not strictly speaking for transportation. General aviation, contrary to popular opinion, is not exclusively non-commercial. Although a large part of general aviation consists of recreational flying, an equally large part involves important commercial activities. General aviation covers a large range of activities both commercial and non-commercial including private flying, flight training, air ambulance, police aircraft, aerial firefighting, air charter, bush flying, gliding, skydiving, and many others. Experimental aircraft, light-sport aircraft and very light jets have emerged in recent years as new trends in general aviation.

Astonishing fact

Seventy-five thousand engineering drawings were used to produce the first Boeing 747.

Military Aviation

Military aviation is used to attack or defend a country through the sky. It includes combat activities as well as flight missions that support military activities.

There are many types of military aircraft, but the basic types of military aircraft are bombers, fighters, spotter planes, transports, patrol aircraft, trainers, and reconnaissance and observation aircraft.

Vehicles of air transport

Hot-air balloons

The first successful type of air transportation that carried humans was the hot air balloon. The Montgolfier brothers developed the idea of designing a large bag or balloon that held hot air in the late 1700s. Passengers and the heat source were placed in a gondola or wicker basket underneath the balloon. Since hot air rises, the balloon flew according to the direction of the wind. By cooling the balloon's temperature, the passengers safely floated back to Earth. Today's hot air balloons use almost the exact same technology; however, they are able to design the balloons into nearly any shape imaginable.

Blimps

An offshoot of the hot air balloon is the blimp. Blimps have been around since the end of the 19th century and were first used as scouting tools by various militaries. The technology has developed into a convenient and cost-effective way to travel and advertise products. To float, blimps use hot air and large fans attached to the gondola underneath. They can be deflated for storage or transportation and inflated cheaply when service is needed. Arguably, the Goodyear Blimp is the most famous of this mode of transportation, seen at sporting games and events around the world.

Astonishing fact

The first United States flight all across the continent occurred in 1911 and took 49 days.

AIR TRANSPORT

Zeppelins

Zeppelins were built in the early 20th century, based on the designs made by Count Ferdinand von Zeppelin. Visually, zeppelins appear very much like blimps. However, they differ on two key points: zeppelins have a metal skeleton with a rigid covering and they are filled with hydrogen. These two elements made zeppelins much larger than blimps and capable of sustaining long-distance flights. During World War I, they were introduced as the first flying machine to practice bombing runs. Through the successive decades, zeppelins were used in the first commercial airline service, ferrying passengers from Germany to the Americas. Unfortunately, the zeppelin industry was destroyed by the public outcry from the 1937 Hindenburg disaster, when a zeppelin exploded over New Jersey, killing 35 people.

Aeroplanes

Aeroplanes are the most popular form of air transportation available. There are around 49,315 commercial flights around the world each day. Nearly 1.1 billion people are flown each year. Aeroplanes are distinguishable from other types of air transportation in that they achieve lift through forward motion. Aeroplanes use a propeller or jet engine to power the aircraft, and the wings act as a stabilizer for keeping the vehicle in the air.

The first design for functional aeroplanes dates back to the 1800s. The first official sustained flight was performed by the Wright Brothers on December 17, 1903. Over the next decade, advances in the technology continued. World War I became the first full-scale testing ground for aeroplanes. Thousands of planes were built for the purpose of spying, bombing and fighting. By the time the war ended, aviation had become a science! Following the war, larger passenger planes were produced, and ultimately, the jet engine was designed, making way for one of the fastest modes of transportation in the world.

Astonishing fact

The tail height of a Boeing 747-400 is equivalent to a six-storey building!

Vehicles of air transport

Helicopters

With the success of the aeroplane, engineers and technicians looked for a way to make the general principles of aeroplanes more efficient. The goal was to develop a flying vehicle that could take off from a sitting position (the position it was without needing a long runway to fly) and carry people to another location. This invention is the helicopter. Helicopters are propelled using horizontal rotors consisting of two or more blades. These blades rotate around the top of the machine, and achieve lift, pulling the body of the helicopter along. Designs for the helicopter had been conceived as far back as the 1480s, by Leonard da Vinci. However, it wasn't until the early 1900s that individuals created working models. The post-war era saw the birth of the helicopter industry. However, most models can only carry four to six people, limiting its commercial use. The primary applications for helicopters are in the military, law enforcement, medical, news or fire control sectors.

Rockets

Perhaps the most advanced form of air transportation comes in the form of rockets. Rockets use thrust obtained via the chemical reaction of a fluid that is ejected at high velocities from the vehicle. The force from the explosion within the vehicle's combustion chamber forces gases out of the tail of the rocket, pushing the vehicle to extremely high speeds. The principle is based on inertia, in that every action has an equal and opposite reaction. Rockets have been used at least since the 13th century for small-scale military applications and recreational displays. However, the first full-scale implementation was during World War II with Germany's V-2 rockets and various rocket-powered aircraft. The post-war era saw the rocket implemented as a mode of transportation that allowed for suborbital and orbital flights in the upper atmosphere. These vehicles are used for both public and private enterprises.

Astonishing fact

An airplane takes off or lands every 37 seconds from Chicago's O'Hare International Airport. That's almost 100 planes per hour!

AIR TRANSPORT

Airport

An airport is a designated location for an aircraft to take off and land. While smaller airports—often called aerodromes, airfields or landing strips—might include short (one or two kilometre) dirt or grass runways, larger airports for international flights normally feature paved runways several kilometres long. Early airports were open grass-covered fields called landing fields, which allowed a pilot to head directly into the wind to aid a plane's lift on takeoff and to decrease its speed on landing. In the 1930s heavier airplanes required paved runway surfaces. Larger planes needed longer runways, which today can reach 4,500 m to accommodate the largest jet aircraft. Air traffic is regulated from control towers and regional centres. Passenger and cargo terminals include baggage-movement and passenger-transit operations.

The essential requirements in airport construction are that the field be as level as possible, that the ground be firm and easily drained, approaches to runways be free of trees, hills, buildings, and other obstructions and that the site be as free as possible of smoke and weather that produces low-visibility conditions. Runways of large airports measure from 762-3,658 m in length and 62-150 m in width. Narrower paved strips called taxiways that connect the runways to other parts of the airport are entered by aircraft as soon as possible after landing, thus freeing the runways for use by other traffic. A taxiway and a runway are usually connected at each end and at several intermediate points. Besides the hangars

Astonishing fact

A plane ticket cost just $5 in the 1920s.

Airport

(buildings for housing and servicing aircraft), airports are usually provided with office and terminal buildings which house administrative, traffic control, communication, and weather observation personnel.

The rapid development of aircraft, especially the jumbo jet and the newer superjumbo jet has created problems for all major airports. Greater speed and weight of aircraft have made longer and more durable runways necessary. Greater numbers of passengers have necessitated more efficient methods of moving people and luggage from curb to plane.

The traffic generated by airports both in the air and on the surface can be a major source of aviation noise and air pollution. The construction of new airports, or addition of runways to existing airports, is often resisted by local residents because of the effect on the countryside, historical sites, local flora and fauna. Locating airports away from densely populated areas can alleviate noise problems, but this solution makes it difficult for passengers and others to reach the airport.

Larger airports may have fixed base operator services, seaplane docks and ramps, air traffic control, passenger facilities such as restaurants and lounges and emergency services. A military airport is known as an airbase or air station. The terms aerodrome, airdrome, airfield and airstrip may also be used to refer to airports, and the terms heliport, seaplane base, and STOLport refer to airports dedicated exclusively to helicopters, seaplanes or short take-off and landing aircrafts.

Astonishing fact

The flight data recorders in airplanes are called 'black boxes,' although they are really bright orange in colour!

Air traffic control (ATC)

The air traffic control system gives guidance to aircraft, to prevent collisions and manage efficient traffic flow.

The task of ensuring safe operations of commercial and private aircraft falls on air traffic controllers. They must coordinate the movements of thousands of aircrafts, keep them at safe distances from each other, direct them during takeoff and landing from airports, direct them around bad weather and ensure that traffic flows smoothly with minimal delays.

When you think about air traffic control, the image of men and women in the tower of an airport probably comes to the mind. However, the air traffic control system is much more complex than that. The movement of aircraft through the various airspace divisions is much like players moving through a 'zone' defence that a basketball or football team might use. As an aircraft travels through a given airspace division, it is monitored by the one or more air traffic controllers responsible for that division. The controllers monitor this plane and give instructions to the pilot. As the plane leaves that airspace division and enters another, the air traffic controller passes it off to the controllers responsible for the new airspace division.

Astonishing fact

The longest time spent airborne during a single hot-air balloon flight is 19 days, 21 hours and 47 minutes!

Advantages of air transport

The advantages of air transport are fast transit times and high quality of service. It is particularly suited to urgent shipments such as medical equipment, newspapers and vital spare parts. Its transit times and reliability of service also has advantages for transporting commodities such as cut flowers, livestock, foodstuffs and pharmaceuticals.

Air transport provides the speediest mode of transport service. The aircraft needs to fly above a certain limit of speed due to the basic aerodynamic principle. Speed is the greatest merit of air transport over land or sea transport. Air transport has brought the world closer and in fact the people can reach the other parts of the world within the shortest possible time. Air transport is used as a very efficient means for speedy transport of men, mail and goods.

In an era where top professionals agree that time is their most valuable resource, air travel is essential to maximizing productivity and ensuring the success of businesses that are becoming less localized each day. A trip that takes days by car or ground transport takes only hours by plane. Since you are not behind the wheel, you also have the ability to multitask while in the air, using travel time to prepare for meetings and fine tune presentations. Or if you are simply a tourist between sights, you can save time by catching up on those travel books and maps before your next destination.

Astonishing fact

An average of 61,000 people are airborne over U.S. at any given hour.

AIR TRANSPORT

This mode of transport does not encounter geographical barriers of the Earth's surface like mountains, hills, deserts, rivers, etc. and this allows air transport to provide faster services. It has also the advantages of linking remote and inaccessible areas across the mountains, oceans, deserts and dense forests.

Technology allows airlines to interact with customers in a more engaging and personalized way. Personalized travel itineraries are sent to your email and cell phone for ready access at airports and destinations. Travel tickets are easy to book online, especially if you are in a rush. Many metropolitan airports are serviced by numerous airlines, making it easier during peak times to book a flight for the dates you want. In addition, most international airports are equipped to serve the wide-ranging needs of travellers. For instance, you should be able to locate hotels or car rental services easily at most major airports for added convenience.

Air travel is also one of the safest modes of transportation that exists today. In 2000, the National Travel Safety Board reported that the number of fatalities caused by road, boating or rail accidents was more common than that of airlines. It is even more dangerous to ride on a bicycle than on an airliner!

Astonishing fact

The 747-400 can carry more than 215,000 litres of fuel, makes it possible to fly extremely long routes, such as Auckland to Los Angeles.

Advantages of air transport

Each day, millions of people book flights in person and online to destinations both domestic and international. Flights leave every half hour from nearly every destination in the world. Air travel is the fastest mode of transportation on the planet. Technology allows customers to quickly research fares, compare prices, use travel-bidding websites, and book flights instantly. Air travel has many advantages in terms of time and quality that make it a very practical means of transportation across the nation and abroad.

Customization of services is an increased focus for airlines. Over the past few years, airlines that once focused primarily on regaining financial stability, are now putting bankruptcies behind them and are re-focusing on their passengers and the overall travel experience. You can expect more choices and options in how, when and where you fly. New innovations in seating, comfort and amenities, especially in the business and first-class cabins are cropping up. Besides having access to the internet, many airlines are also offering more in-flight services and entertainment. Your travel considerations maybe less about whether you should travel by air or not, but whether you should choose Airline 1 or Airline 2.

In the future, another advantage of airline travel maybe environmental. Many airlines are starting to go green and are seeking alternatives to petroleum based fuels.

> The fewest airplane passengers killed in one year was 1 in 1993 and the most was 583 in 1977 when two Boeing 747s collided on the runway at Los Rodeos airport, Tenerife, the Canary Islands.

AIR TRANSPORT

Disadvantages of air transport

It needs a large terminal area that maybe some distance from the destination it serves.

It is expensive due to the large amounts of power expended and the high safety standards demanded.

Another disadvantage associated with air transportation is its lack of accessibility. Since a plane cannot ordinarily be pulled up to a loading dock, it is necessary to bring products to and from the airport by truck.

It has negative environmental impacts. Most forms of aviation release carbon dioxide and other greenhouse gases into the Earth's atmosphere, contributing to the acceleration of global warming.

Air transport is particularly vulnerable to terrorism and to fluctuating fuel prices.

In 1913, the Russian Airline became the first to introduce a toilet on board.

Role in economic development

Air transport facilitates links to inaccessible areas. It aids land transport in the economic development of areas where other means of transport is practically absent. In regions where road cannot be constructed or land transportation links cannot be established, this mode of transport is to be pressed into service because of necessity. Settlement in various mining areas or in the snow-fed areas is only possible because of air transportation links.

Air transport helps to expand the geographical market. Air transport has prompted a number of industries to expand their geographical markets and introduce innovative distribution technique. The globalization of production market has contributed significantly to the growth of air transport. Now the supply of international market is provided by some three hundred airlines.

It creates consumer market. Despite the fact that air transportation has been expensive, all the nations have utilized every opportunity in developing this mode of transport. The development of civil aviation has been due to the desire to have well organized air-routes to reach the consumer market. Air cargo has created new markets and has contributed notably to the development of international trade in certain high cost commodities.

> Man's first known attempt at flight dates back to 1020, when Oliver of Malmesbury, an English Benedictine monk, strapped a huge pair of wings to his body and endeavoured to soar into the air from Malmesbury Abbey. He fell and broke both his legs.

AIR TRANSPORT

Air transport helps to increase military importance. Aircrafts are not merely the carrier of goods or passenger or mail but they are also used as weapons of war. They maintain a system of high-speed transportation requirement of the government and of essential industry in war as well as in peace. The most important advantage military aviation derives from civil aviation is in the development of airways, air navigational aids and ground organization. The military importance of air transport generally prompts the governments to attach more importance for the development of this sector. Air transport serves the border areas to strengthen national security.

Air transport industries also create employment opportunities. Development of civil aviation offers jobs in its different segments of operation. Skilled and unskilled persons can be employed in a larger scale with better co-ordination of road and air transport.

It provides faster relief operations during

flood, cyclone, drought and other natural calamities. When all the land routes of a particular place are cut-off due to natural and other calamities, air transport is the only means to connect that area. Air surveys can also be undertaken to know the topography of a region by using helicopters. In times of drought, artificial rain can also be made by aircrafts.

Astonishing fact

Concorde, which was retired from service in 2003, is the fastest commercial airplane. It travels over 11 miles above the Earth— so high that you can see the curve of the Earth!

Role in economic development

Air transport assists in increasing foreign exchange reserve. A national airline can help in saving foreign exchange. Receipts from foreign travellers, export freight and airport expenditure by foreign airlines provide revenues of great value in terms of foreign exchange for many airliners. The wide-ranging opportunities offered by long-haul aircrafts attract tourists. Its related economic benefits are enjoyed by smaller and less developed countries. Economic gains are achieved by the use of air transport as a stimulant to trade, tourism and industry and the location of one or more international airport terminals in the vicinity of a capital city is a factor critical to national growth.

It assists in developing international tourism by offering attractive travel package to the travellers. The hotel industry can grow with the development of better airport facilities and frequencies of air services. The growth of floriculture industries is possible because of fast transportation facilities through air services. Speedy delivery of these types of products is required because of its perishable nature and air transport fulfills this condition.

Air transport reduces the transit time of transportation, which is vital to boost economic activities. Trading, commercial and official activities can be done at the quickest possible time because of availability of air transport. Better international understanding is essential for the welfare of the human race. This requires frequent visit of top dignitaries of a country to the other country to assemble in an international summit and this is possible because of availability of air transport.

Astonishing fact

In only eight minutes, the Space Shuttle can accelerate to a speed of 27,000 km/h.

AIR TRANSPORT

Limitations of air transport services

Air services are affected by adverse weather conditions. Weather condition of a region plays an important part in setting up an airport. In earlier days of air transport, this natural factor played an important role. However, with the development of air flight technology, the airplane can fly at a higher level, thus avoiding the weather hazard. Further, development of radio technology, introduction of modern technical equipment for night flying, considerably reduced the weather hazards. However, other weather hazards such as cloud, fog, smoke, dust storm either interfere with the visibility or affect performance of the air transport service.

The rate of obsolescence and depreciation in respect of aircraft is very high. Cost of replacing outdated aircraft requires appropriation from profit each year to reduce burden on the management of the airlines.

> The biggest helicopter was the Russian Mil Mi-12 Homer of 1968 which could lift 40,204 kg up to 2255 m.

It is not popular for bulk freight transport. As regards freight, it is a popular means of transport, except for commodities of high value per unit of weight, like costly medicines, perishable product and electronic products, etc. The commodities, which can withstand high transport cost, are generally transported by air. It also cannot provide doorstep services or direct connectivity to consumption points.

Air transportation is not advantageous or economical over short distances. It is because of this unavoidable limitation that all domestic airlines running for short distances have either been abandoned or are heavily subsidized by Governments.

Limitations of air transport services

Air transport development requires huge capital investment. Traffic control building has to be constructed for safe landing of aircrafts. Provisions for ground facilities like air traffic control, radio and meteorological services with modern technical equipment is essential for air transport development. A large area is required for the construction of aerodrome to accommodate large sized aircraft and this requires a sizable investment. An aircraft is costly to manufacture, costly to operate and costly to maintain. It needs very high consumption of energy per unit of weight carried.

Many countries impose several legal restrictions on foreign airliners in the interest of their own national unity and peace.

Air transport can only be availed by the rich and affluent classes of a society because of its high freight cost. This means only the privileged class of the society can avail this opportunity. Air transport presently is a luxury in the developing countries. Only a small fraction of the total population uses this service.

Its cargo and passenger carrying capacity is low as compared to road, rail and water transport.

Air travel is risky. The chances of breakdown due to various factors are high and the chance of survival in case of any accident during the journey is very remote.

There are more than 15,000 civil helicopters operating in more than 157 other countries around the world.

AIR TRANSPORT

Famous aircraft manufacturers

Airbus

Airbus is one of the world's leading aircraft manufacturers. Airbus is based in Europe with its headquarters in Toulouse, France and has 12 sites in Europe located in France, Germany, Spain and UK. They employ about 52,000 people from 85 nationalities who speak among them over 20 different languages. Airbus currently has a product line-up of 14 jet aircraft types which range from 100 to 525 seats. There has been more than 9,200 aircraft ordered throughout the world as the Airbus aircraft family is recognised for its comfort, economics and versatility. The company produces around half of the world's jet airliners. The company is known for producing and marketing the world's largest airliner, the A380.

Boeing

Boeing is the world's leading aerospace company and the largest manufacturer of commercial jetliners and military aircraft combined. Additionally, Boeing designs and manufactures rotorcraft, electronic and defense systems, missiles, satellites, launch vehicles and advanced information and communication systems. As a major service provider to NASA, Boeing operates the Space Shuttle and International Space Station. The company also provides numerous military and commercial airline support services. Boeing is based in USA with its headquarters located in Chicago. They employ more than 158,000 people across the United States and in 70 countries, making them one of the most diverse, talented and innovative workforces anywhere in the world. The main commercial product that Boeing manufacturers are the 737, 747, 767 and 777 families of aeroplanes and the Boeing Business Jet, with nearly 12,000 commercial jetliners in service worldwide (about 75 per cent of the world fleet).

Famous aircraft manufacturers

Embraer

Embraer has become one of the main aircraft manufacturers in the world by focusing on specific market segments with high growth potential in commercial, defence, and executive aviation. Headquartered in São José dos Campos, Embraer is, alongside Canadian rival Bombardier, the third-largest commercial aircraft company in the world and currently employ more than 17,237 people. Embraer continues to lead the industry with its innovative regional and commercial jet product lines. Since 1996, Embraer has produced and delivered more than 1000 aircrafts to more than 37 airlines in 24 countries.

Bombardier

The world's third largest civil aircraft manufacturer, Bombardier is a leader in the design and manufacture of innovative aviation products and services for the business, regional and amphibious aircraft markets. Headquartered in Montréal, Canada, Bombardier employs more than 28,000 people worldwide. With a legacy that consolidates more than 250 years of aviation history, they boast a stellar product portfolio. Their business jets, regional jets, turboprops and amphibious firefighters are celebrated worldwide for their reliable, superior performance. In addition, each aircraft has the support of world-class Bombardier technical and maintenance services.

Its industry-leading business aircraft, including the renowned Learjet, Challenger and Global business jet families, cover 97 per cent of the business aircraft market.

AIR TRANSPORT

Largest air transport crafts

Antonov An-225

Antonov AN-225 is the world's heaviest and largest jet ever built with the landing gear system of 32 wheels and a wing span of 291 feet. Originally built in 1988 to carry the Russian Buran space shuttle, this mission disappeared when the Soviet Union dissolved and their space program was drastically cut back.

It is capable of carrying ultra-heavy and oversize freight, up to 250,000 kg internally or 200,000 kg on the upper fuselage, such as locomotives and 150-ton generators, and has become a valuable asset to international relief organizations for its ability to quickly transport huge quantities of emergency supplies during disaster relief operations.

The first flight was on December 21, 1988. However, after the collapse of the Soviet Union the Buran space shuttle program was cancelled and in 1994 the single An-225 built was grounded. It was kept in storage in Ukraine until 2000. Then Antonov revived the aircraft and upgraded it with new avionics and other new equipment. The renewed An-225 started flying again on May 7, 2001 and made its first commercial flight on 3 January 2003 from Stuttgart in Germany to Thumrait in Oman. It is operated by Antonov Airlines, as a commercial transport for outsize and heavy cargo loads.

During the 1980s Antonov started the construction of a second An-225, but the work stopped in 1994. The aircraft is kept in storage, however, and Antonov considers the completion of the second aircraft if market conditions justify the investment.

Largest air transport crafts

Airbus A380

Airbus' 21st Century flagship A380 has been revolutionising air transport since its service introduction in 2007, bringing unmatched performance and economic efficiency to airline customers worldwide.

The double-deck A380 is the world's largest commercial aircraft flying today, with capacity to carry 525 passengers in a comfortable three-class configuration, and up to 853 in a single-class configuration that provides wider seats than its competitor. Overall, the A380's two decks offer 50 per cent more floor surface than any other high-capacity aircraft.

In addition to offering unequalled levels of passenger comfort, the A380 provides the lowest fuel burn per seat – which allows airlines to substantially reduce CO_2 emissions while achieving profitable, sustainable growth for decades to come.

It also is the quietest long-haul aircraft flying today, generating 50 per cent less noise on departure than the nearest competitor, as well as three to four time less when landing, all while carrying 40 per cent more passengers.

AIR TRANSPORT

Boeing 747-8

The Boeing 747, first flown in 1969, is the largest commercial airliner, flying the farthest, and carrying the greatest number of passengers of any airliner. It has approximately 6 million parts.

The 747-8 is the largest and newest 747 version, the longest passenger aircraft in the world. The 747-8 is offered in two main variants: the 747-8 Intercontinental (747-8I) for passengers and the 747-8 Freighter (747-8F) for cargo. The aircraft will be capable of carrying up to 467 passengers in a 3-class configuration over 15,000 km at Mach 0.855.

The 747-8 Intercontinental will have the lowest seat-mile cost of any large commercial jetliner, with 12 per cent lower costs than its predecessor, the 747-400.

The aeroplane provides 16 per cent better fuel economy, 16 per cent less carbon emissions per passenger and generates a 30 per cent smaller noise footprint than the 747-400.

Antonov An-124 Ruslan

The Antonov An-124 is a big four-engine cargo aircraft, suitable for carrying outsize and very heavy payloads up to 150 tons (330.000 lb). It is the world's largest ever serially-manufactured cargo airplane and world's second largest operating cargo aircraft.

The An-124 'Ruslan' is designed by the Ukrainian aircraft manufacturer Antonov that is well-known as the maker of the biggest and heaviest aircraft in the world. In the 1960s it developed the An-22 turboprop, which was the biggest aircraft in the world at that time. It was followed by the An-124 Ruslan and later the An-225 Mriya, a stretched version of the An-124 and the biggest operational aircraft in the world at the moment.

The Antonov An-124 was primarily developed as a strategic military transport aircraft in the same class as the American Lockheed C-5A Galaxy, but today it is mainly used as a civil cargo aircraft. The An-124 and the C-5A look much the same. The main visual difference is that the Antonov has a low tail and the Galaxy a so-called T-tail. In its military role it is intended to transport tanks, missiles and other heavy equipment. As a civil cargo aircraft the An-124 flies loads like hydraulic turbines, locomotives, big crane trucks, aircraft fuselages, helicopters and even sea yachts. The aircraft has set some dozens of world records.

AIR TRANSPORT

Lockheed C-5 Galaxy

The Lockheed C-5 Galaxy is a four-engine heavy military transport aircraft with a maximum payload of 122.472 kg (270.000 lbs) produced by the US-American manufacturer Lockheed Corporation, today Lockheed Martin Aeronautics Company. The Lockheed C-5 Galaxy is one of the largest military aircraft operating in the world today.

The C-5 Galaxy was presented to the United States Air Force, for training purposes, in December 1969. The first operational aircraft were delivered to the 437th Military Airlift Wing (MAW), Charleston AFB, SC, in June 1970.

The Lockheed-Georgia C-5 Galaxy can carry 135 tons of cargo, making it the largest production aircraft built in the United States and a vital part of any military action in which large amounts of material need to be airlifted around the world. It has a wingspan of just less than 68m and is 75 m long and 20 m high. It has four engines; each engine pod is nearly 8 m long. Until the release of the Soviet Antonov An-124 Condor in 1982, the C-5 was the largest and heaviest plane in operation.

The plane was designed for carrying large amounts of cargo and personnel. Its upper deck can carry ninety-six passengers and crew members. At both ends of the aircraft large doors can swing open to the cargo deck, and two rows of vehicles can drive on and off at the same time. This lower cargo deck can carry a wide range of cargoes, such as a seventy-four-ton folding mobile scissors bridge; or two M1-A1 Abrams main battle tanks; or seven UH-1 Huey helicopters; or 270 personnel (reserved for emergencies and special operations); or 135 tons of cargo.

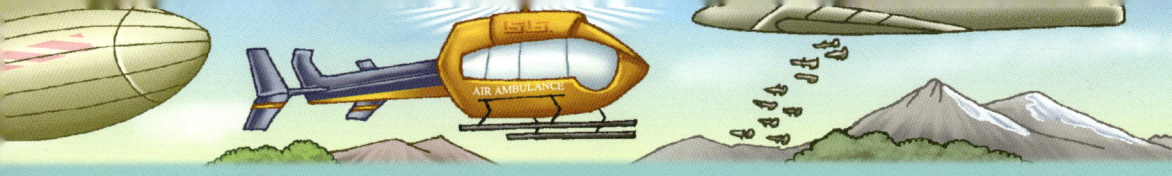

Test Your MEMORY

1. What do you mean by air transport?

2. Describe briefly the history of air transport.

3. Name the types of air transport.

4. Define the types of air transport vehicles.

5. What is an airport?

6. What is Air Traffic Control (ATC)?

7. What are the advantages of air transport?

8. What are the disadvantages of air transport?

9. Write the role of air transport in economic development.

10. Write the limitations of air transport services.

11. Name some famous aircraft manufacturers.

12. Name some famous aircrafts.

AIR TRANSPORT

Index

A

aerodromes 12
Aeronautique Internationale 5
aeroplanes 3, 10, 11, 24
airbase 13
Airbus 24, 27
Airbus A380 27
aircraft 3, 7, 8, 10, 11, 12, 13, 14, 15, 22, 23, 24, 25, 26, 27, 28, 29, 30
airfields 12
air mail 7
Airport 11, 12, 13, 14, 17, 18, 21, 22
airstrip 13
air traffic control 13, 14, 23
Antonov An-124 Ruslan 29
Antonov An-225 26
atmosphere 3, 11, 18

B

barnstormers 5
beacons 3
blimps 9, 10
Boeing 5, 7, 8, 10, 17, 24, 28
Boeing 747-8 28
Bombardier 25

C

Cargolux 7
commercial aviation 7

E

Embraer 25

G

general aviation 7, 8
gliders 4
Gustave whitehead 5

H

helicopters 5, 11, 13, 20, 23, 29, 30
heliport 13
hot air balloons 4, 9

J

jet planes 5

K

kites 4

L

Learjet 25
Lockheed C-5 Galaxy 30

M

military aviation 7, 8, 20
Montgolfier brothers 4, 9

R

radio beams 3
rockets 11
runway 10, 11, 12, 17

S

seaplane base 13
sea planes 4
STOLport 13

T

taxiways 12
Tupolev Tu-104 5

W

Wright Brothers 4, 5, 6, 10

Z

zeppelins 10

PEGASUS ENCYCLOPEDIA LIBRARY

Transport
CARS

Edited by: Pallabi B. Tomar
Managing editor: Tapasi De
Designed by: Vijesh Chahal, Anil Kumar and Rohit Kumar
Illustrated by: Suman S. Roy, Tanoy Choudhury
Colouring done by: Vinay Kumar, Sonu, Kiran Kumari & Pradeep Kumar

CARS

CONTENTS

Introduction 3

History of cars 4

Production of cars 7

Parts of a car 9

Advantages of cars 13

Disadvantages 15

Cost and maintenance 16

Industry 20

Future car technologies 21

Some famous automobile makers 23

Some famous cars 27

Test Your Memory 31

Index 32

Introduction

By definition an automobile or car is a wheeled vehicle that carries its own motor and transports passengers. Most definitions of the term specify that automobiles are designed to run primarily on roads, to have seating for one to eight people, to typically have four wheels, and to be constructed principally for the transport of people rather than goods.

The automobile as we know it was not invented in a single day by a single inventor. The history of the automobile reflects an evolution that took place worldwide. It is estimated that over 100,000 patents created the modern automobile.

There are approximately 600 million passenger cars worldwide (roughly one car per eleven people). Around the world, there were about 806 million cars and light trucks on the road in 2007; they burn over a billion cubic metres (260 billion US gallons) of petrol/gasoline and diesel fuel yearly. The numbers are increasing rapidly, especially in China and India.

The first Japanese car in the United States was the Honda Accord manufactured in November 1982.

CARS

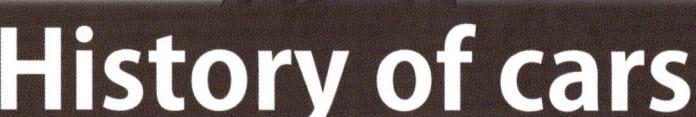

History of cars

In terms of the lives of average people, there is little doubt that the automobile is the most revolutionary invention in the history of transportation since the wheel. The basic premise of the automobile is simple; choose a wheeled vehicle from the many types typically pulled by horses or oxen, add a motor and create a self-propelled, personal transportation vehicle. The earliest ancestor of the modern automobile is probably the Fardier, a three-wheeled, steam-powered, 2.3-mph vehicle built in 1771 by **Nicolas Joseph Cugnot** for the French minister of war. This cumbersome machine was never put into production because it was much slower and harder to operate than a horse-drawn vehicle.

Amedee Bollee, also a Frenchman, built an improved 12-passenger steam car in 1873, but the steam engine proved impractical for a machine that was intended to challenge the speed of a horse-and-buggy. The invention of the practical automobile had to await the invention of a workable internal combustion engine.

In 1807 **Francois Isaac de Rivaz** designed the first internal combustion engine. This was subsequently used by him to develop the world's first vehicle to run on such an engine, one that used a mixture of hydrogen and oxygen to generate energy.

> The first cars used lever instead of steering wheel.

History of cars

This spawned the birth of a number of designs based on the internal combustion engine in the early nineteenth century with little or no degree of commercial success. In 1860 thereafter, **Jean Joseph Etienne Lenoir** built the first successful two-stroke gas driven engine. In 1862 he again built an experimental vehicle driven by his gas-engine, which ran at a speed of 3 km/hr. These cars became popular and by 1865 could be frequently espied on the roads. The next major leap forward occurred in 1885 when the four stroke engine was devised. The milestone vehicle was built in Germany in 1889 by **Gottlieb Daimler** and **Wilhelm Maybach**. Powered by a 1.5 hp, two-cylinder gasoline engine, it had a four-speed transmission and travelled at 10 mph.

Another German, **Karl Benz**, also built a gasoline-powered car the same year. The gasoline-powered automobile or motor car, remained largely a curiosity for the rest of the nineteenth century, with only a handful being manufactured in Europe and the United States. The first automobile to be produced in quantity was the 1901 Curved Dash Oldsmobile, which was built in the United States by Ransom E. Olds. Modern automobile mass production and its use of the modern industrial assembly line, is credited to Henry Ford of Detroit, Michigan, who had built his first gasoline-powered car in 1896. Ford began producing his Model T in 1908, and by 1927, when it was discontinued; over 18 million cars had been sold off.

Ferrari makes a maximum of 14 cars every day.

CARS

Some of the major breakthroughs in the automobile history are as follows:

- 1769: Nicholas Joseph Cugnot (1725-1804) from France built the first self-propelled road vehicle (military tractor) for the French Army. It was a three-wheeled vehicle with a maximum speed of 2.5 mph.

- 1832-1839: Robert Anderson, from Scotland built the first electric carriage.

- 1885/86: Karl Friedrich Benz (1844-1929) from Germany built the first true automobile. This three-wheeled vehicle was powered by an internal combustion engine. The engine was a four-stroke one and it formed a single unit along with the chassis.

- 1886: Gottileb Wilhelm Daimler (1834-1900) and Wilhelm Maybach (1846-1929) built the first gasoline powered, four-wheeled, four-stroke engine which is also known as the Cannstatt-Daimler.

- 1876-95: George Baldwin Selden (1846-1922) combined the internal combustion engine with a carriage. This vehicle was also powered by gasoline.

- 1893: Charles Edgar Duryea (1862-1938) and his brother Frank Duryea (1870-1967) from United States built the first successful gasoline powered car. This car had a 4 HP, 2-stroke motor.

In 1887, Benz was the first car company to be offered for sale.

Production of cars

Production of cars

By the early 1900s, gasoline cars started to outsell all other types of motor vehicles. The market was growing for economical automobiles and the need for industrial production was pressing.

The first car manufacturers in the world were French: Panhard & Levassor (1889) and Peugeot (1891). By car manufacturer we mean builders of entire motor vehicles for sale and not just engine inventors who experimented with car design to test their engines. Daimler and Benz began as the latter before becoming full car manufacturers and made their early money by licensing their patents and selling their engines to car manufacturers.

America's first gasoline-powered commercial car manufacturers were Charles and Frank Duryea. The brothers were bicycle makers who became interested in gasoline engines and automobiles and built their first motor vehicle in 1893, in Springfield, Massachusetts. By 1896, the Duryea Motor Wagon Company had sold thirteen models of the Duryea, an expensive limousine, which remained in production into the 1920s.

Astonishing fact

The fastest time for removing a car engine, and replacing it is 42 seconds for a Ford Escort, on November 21, 1985.

7

CARS

The first automobile to be mass produced in the United States was the 1901 Curved Dash Oldsmobile, built by the American car manufacturer **Ransom Eli Olds** (1864-1950). Olds invented the basic concept of the assembly line and started the Detroit area automobile industry. He first began making steam and gasoline engines with his father, Pliny Fiske Olds, in Lansing, Michigan in 1885. Olds designed his first steam-powered car in 1887. In 1899, with a growing experience of gasoline engines, Olds moved to Detroit to start the Olds Motor Works, and produce low-priced cars. He produced 425 'Curved Dash Olds' in 1901, and was America's leading auto manufacturer from 1901 to 1904.

American car manufacturer, **Henry Ford** (1863-1947) invented an improved assembly line and installed the first conveyor belt-based assembly line in his car factory in Ford's Highland Park, Michigan plant, around 1913-14. The assembly line reduced production costs for cars by reducing assembly time. Ford's famous Model T was assembled in ninety-three minutes. Ford made his first car, called the 'Quadricycle,' in June, 1896. However, success came after he formed the Ford Motor Company in 1903. This was the third car manufacturing company formed to produce the cars he designed. He introduced the Model T in 1908 and it was a success. After installing the moving assembly lines in his factory in 1913, Ford became the world's biggest car manufacturer. By 1927, 15 million Model Ts had been manufactured.

Another victory won by **Henry Ford** was patent battle with George B. Selden. Selden, who had never built an automobile, held a patent on a 'road engine', on that basis Selden was paid royalties by all American car manufacturers. Ford's victory saved the american manufacturer from paying royalties to Selden. He also ushered in the age of inexpensive cars with his Model T.

Astonishing fact

The world's longest traffic hold-up was 110 miles long, between Paris and Lyon on the French Autoroute in 1980. A more recent contender for the title was a 100 mile long traffic jam, near Hamburg in Germany in 1993.

8

Parts of a car

A car is a complex machine with several systems functioning simultaneously. While most modern cars contain computerized systems that are beyond the understanding of all but the most specialized technicians, knowing the basic parts of a car and how they function makes it easier to spot problems, perform basic repairs and drive more responsibly.

Engine

Every car is powered by an engine, and most cars use an internal combustion engine that runs on gasoline. Gas, along with air, is drawn into a combustion chamber where it is compressed and ignited by a spark. The resulting combustion provides a power stroke that, when repeated rapidly, powers the car. Engines are often referred to by the number of cylinders they have, and each cylinder contains its own combustion chamber. A car's overall power is a function of the size of the engine as well as factors such as the timing of the combustion and the type of transmission used.

Astonishing fact

Luxembourg has the most crowded roads in Europe with 570 cars per 1,000 people!

Driveline

The driveline is a series of components that connect the motion produced by the engine to the wheels of the car to provide forward (or backward) motion. The engine is connected to a drive shaft (a rigid metal shaft) via the transmission. Whether a car uses an automatic or manual transmission, the function is the same; to use metal gears to match the engine's speed to the power requirements of the car, which depend on vehicle speed, the slope of the road surface and the weight of the car itself. Additional gears transmit power from the drive shaft to the wheels themselves.

Engine

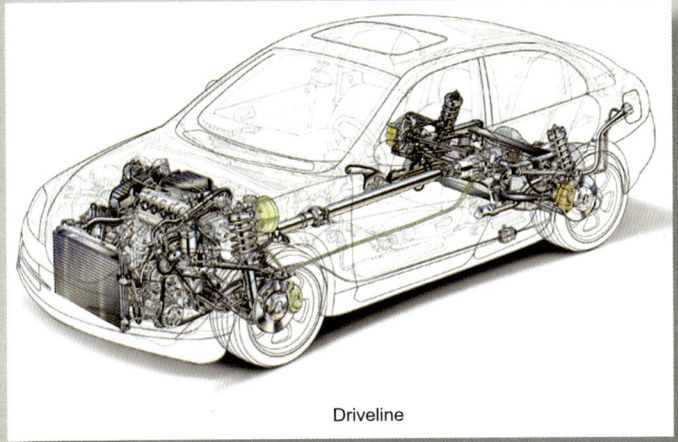
Driveline

CARS

Electrical system

A car's electrical system is powered by a rechargeable battery that draws its power from the engine itself, which acts as a generator. The battery is used to start the car, providing the initial motion of the engine and powering items such as the fuel pump and starter. A car's battery is also used to power the headlights, radio, dashboard gauges, turn signals and an array of safety sensors. Most cars also have additional uses for the electrical system such as power automatic windows or door locks. All of these electrical items are wired to the battery with a series of fuses ensuring that the electrical system can continue to function even if one part fails.

Astonishing fact

In 1924 a Ford automobile cost $265.

Brakes and wheels

Various types of wheels and tires are useful for driving under specific conditions. All-season tires, for example, have the versatility of being used throughout the year, even if severe conditions occur. A car's brakes are one of its most important safety features and generally come in one of two types— disc or drum. Disc brakes use a spinning disc, which is pinched between brake pads mounted on callipers to slow the motion of the car. Drum brakes use shoes that push outward to contact the inside of a spinning cylinder or drum. Some cars contain both types of brakes (one type for the front wheels, another for the rear wheels) to take advantage of the best each type of braking system has to offer.

Brakes

Electrical system

Wheels

10

Parts of a car

Chassis

The chassis of the car contains the skeletal frame of the car. The most notable components of the chassis are the steering system, which allows you to turn the wheels and change direction; the suspension system, which keeps the wheels on the ground, prevents a bumpy ride and stabilizes the steering; the frame that supports all the car's parts and keeps them together, and the wheels.

Chassis

Dashboard instruments

One of the most visible parts of a car is its instrumentation. Most drivers are aware of the speedometer and fuel gauge, but other dashboard instruments are equally important. A tachometer, which displays engine speed in rotations per minute

> The windshield wipers, which are an important component of every car, were introduced by a woman.

(RPM), indicates how hard the engine is working. An oil pressure gauge or engine temperature gauge can be useful in diagnosing common problems, such as a leak of oil or engine coolant respectively. Stopping a car when oil pressure begins to drop or temperature begins to rise can avoid catastrophic engine failure.

Body

Much engineering goes into designing the car's body, which is composed of the metal, plastic or fibreglass pieces that cover the hood, roof, doors and sides of the car. It also includes the bumpers, windows, grille and trunk lid. The design of the car body must attempt to minimize drag to increase fuel efficiency, as well as be aesthetically appealing to the driver.

Dashboard instruments

Body

11

CARS

Some other basic parts of a car are—

Radiator helps to remove heat from the cooling system as coolant, which absorbs the heat from the engine, passes through it.

Muffler reduces the noise emitted by the exhaust of cars. You will notice a radical difference in the noise level of a vehicle with a muffler and a car without.

Battery supplies the initial burst of electrical power that starts the engine.

Alternator is the alternative to the battery; it recharges the battery and supplies power to all electrical components while the engine is running.

Suspension system receives all the shock and jolts from the roads, keeping the wheels of the vehicle on the ground as much as possible. Leaf springs are a type of suspension that are used by many to stabilize their vehicles, especially for those carrying heavy load.

Ford Motor Company only made 107 models of the Ford GT40 of which 7 were on road cars.

Alternator

Battery

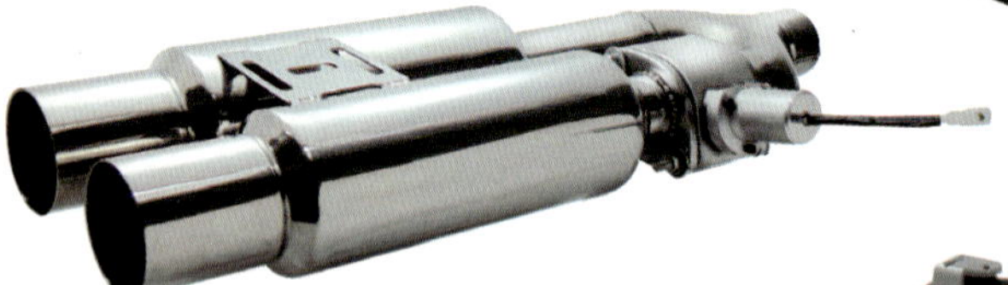

Muffler

Radiator

Suspension system

The world's cheapest car is manufactured in India and is called the 'TATA Nano'.

Advantages of cars

Transportation

Transportation is the main advantage of buying a car. If you don't own your own vehicle, you are dependent on walking, biking, asking others to give you a ride or taking cabs or public transportation. When you have your own car, you can go wherever you want, whenever you want, without being dependent on anyone else. Cars can be considered an addition to personal freedom.

Employment

Buying a car can help you get or maintain your job. If you don't have a vehicle and depend on others to drive you to work, you have a greater chance of arriving late. If that happens too often, it may count against you badly enough to affect your performance reviews or even get you fired. With your own car you are in control of getting to work. More jobs are available because of the rapid growth of automobiles in the world.

Safety

When you buy a car, you gain a big safety advantage. People who walk or bike are at a greater risk of everything from getting rained on to getting robbed to being struck by a vehicle. When you are in a car, you don't have as many worries about the weather or being attacked by others. It maybe harder to drive in the rain, but you are protected inside the vehicle. Someone can try to carjack you, and you can get into an accident, but your odds are much better than being unprotected on foot or on a bike.

CARS

Prestige

Buying a car may help you make a better impression on other people. When you can say that you are a car owner, it gives a sense of responsibility, stability and financial security. When you don't have a vehicle, people might speculate that you don't have a good job or that your credit rating is low.

Economic value

Doubtlessly cars have an enormous economic value. Without the automobile and derivations like trucks, the productivity of a modern economy would seriously be affected. The biggest part of transportation of goods is still conducted by trucks. But the automobile does not only contribute to modern economies as a means of transportation. It also has profound effects on the availability and distribution of working places. Having a car largely increases a family's mobility and flexibility. Because of the possibility to commute the advantages of life on the countryside can still be enjoyed while being occupied in an urban region.

This is also a part of the change in lifestyle made by the spreading of the automobile. Children can now be raised in a non-urban environment even if their parents work in the city centre. Cars may also contribute to a strengthening of family ties especially if the members live in distant regions. It maybe much more agreeable to cover distances by a car than by other means of transportation.

> **Hong Kong has the most Rolls Royce cars per person.**

Disadvantages

The invention of the automobile was without doubt one of the most groundbreaking advancements in human technology. Today we cannot imagine a world without it anymore. A large portion of our everyday life is dominated by cars! The noise they produce, the streets built for them or the possibilities they offer are always a part of our perception.

On the other hand, cars are linked to a variety of problems. The most important of which are environmental ones. Cars are one of the biggest contributors to all kinds of pollution. A large proportion of the total amount of carbon dioxide produced by humans originates from the use of cars. Thus they contribute to the depletion of the ozone layer as well as to global warming. They also add to the pollution of densely inhabited regions by producing noise and as the main factor in the widespread phenomena called 'smog'.

Furthermore taking into account the yearly number of deaths in traffic it is obvious that cars also produce a lot of problems which have to be tackled in order to fully enjoy this invention.

Astonishing fact

The automobile is the most recycled product in the world.

Cost and maintenance

There is so much to do with a car, when it comes to maintenance. Right from a small job of checking tire pressure to a comprehensive overhauling, car maintenance costs vary in a very wide range. Here are some common tasks that make up the maintenance cost of cars.

Car wash

Although it is the simplest and cheapest car job, it must be mentioned as a type of car maintenance.

Car air conditioner

Air conditioner is an integral part of any car, taking care of the comfort of the passengers. Proper functioning of the air conditioner is definitely a thing of importance for the comfort of the occupants of the car. While driving in hot and humid weather, an efficient air conditioner is a must.

Car brakes

Brakes are, of course, the most vital safety component of a car, and it is mandatory for your own security that you keep the brakes of your car in good condition. Brake problems do not rise to a serious level suddenly. Most brake problems develop gradually and if the system is detected properly, these can be remedied before they become serious.

Car cooling system

Cooling system in a car protects the engine from overheating. One must always use good quality coolant for car engine. The coolant level must be checked at least once a fortnight.

> The first speeding tickets were given out in 1902, when the top speed of most cars was around 72 km per hour.

Cost and maintenance

Car engine

When it comes to a car, the most important component is the engine. The engine can well be regarded as the soul of a car. In fact, you might have the most maintained and sparkling set of wheels in your neighbourhood, but if the engine is not working, everything is a waste! In order to make sure that your car has a long life, check any irregularities in the engine at regular intervals.

Car fuel system

One of the basic components of a car comprises of its engine and talking about

The first road traffic death happened in 1896 when a lady died after getting hit by a passing car.

the car engine, its fuel system needs to properly taken care of. In fact, proper car maintenance is incomplete without adequate maintenance of the fuel system.

Car gears

Gear system forms an important component of a car and thus, requires proper handling and attention on your part. Since they help you maintain the speed of your car; you cannot afford to misuse the gears.

Car tyres

Though a large number of car owners are unaware of the fact, car tyres have an important bearing on the performance and safety of the car. In fact, when car maintenance is the question in point, ensuring a good condition of the tyres is an issue that occupies a central place.

CARS

Car alternator

The alternator produces electricity used to maintain battery storage charge and to help run all the electrical accessories, including the ignition and the engine control systems. It is belt-driven by the engine and produces an alternating current (AC), which is converted internally to 12 volts direct current (DC) by the diode bridge or rectifiers.

Car battery

The battery acts as the nerve centre of a car's entire electrical system. It stores energy produced by the alternator or generator and supplies it to those systems requiring smooth, uninterrupted and continuous current (lights, fuel injection system, main computer). There are several types of batteries used in modern automobiles.

The first car radio was invented in the year 1929; it was called 'Motorola'.

Car starter

Car starter is simply a DC motor that turns the engine crankshaft through the flywheel, starting the combustion process by creating compression within the cylinders. Voltage to the starter is supplied directly from the battery and is controlled by a relay and/or solenoid operated from the key switch inside your car.

Air filter

Having a properly working air filter is one of the key factors in gas mileage. If you have a clog in your filter, your gas mileage will plummet and your car could frequently stall. Air filters should be

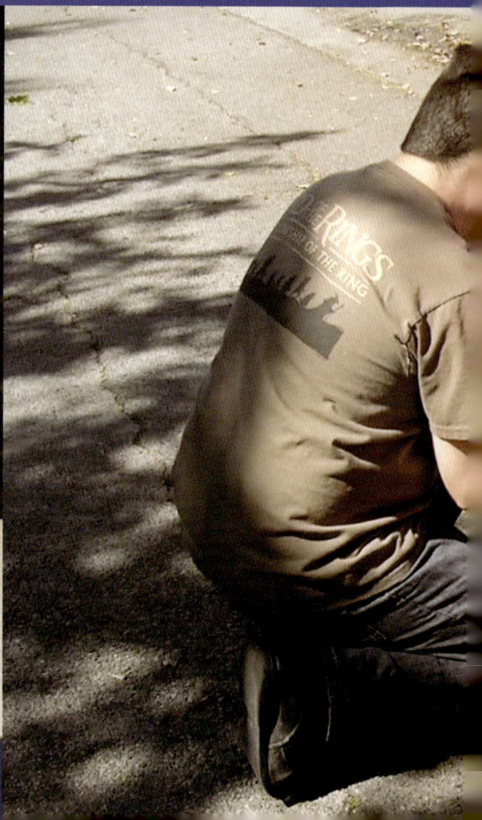

Cost and maintenance

replaced every 15,000 miles. This is a fairly simple procedure that costs little.

Antifreeze

Water and antifreeze run through hoses in the engine to cool it off. Part of your routine car maintenance should be to check the antifreeze level before the winter season. Antifreeze will prevent water from freezing in your hoses.

Brake fluid

Brake fluid should be replaced every 2 years. Each time you change your oil (about every 3 months), check the brake fluid level. You will be able to tell if your fluid is low because your brakes will become spongy.

Power steering

Power steering is made possible with

Astonishing fact

On an average, human beings spend around 2 weeks of their time waiting for traffic lights to turn green.

power steering fluid. You should check to make sure your power steering fluid is full every 6 months. If you are going on a long trip, check before you leave.

Car maintenance is very important to our lifestyles. Vehicles allow us to travel to work and earn a living. You must make sure you properly maintain your car so that it lasts as long as possible.

CARS

Industry

Automobile industry includes designs, manufacture and development and selling of motor vehicles such as two wheelers, three wheelers, cars, trucks, buses, tractors and other vehicles. It is one of the most important sectors of the world in terms of revenue collection.

Today, automobile industry is an emerging sector. Every year lots of companies launch different models of cars, bikes and other vehicles suiting the taste of the consumers. Automobile industry is occupied by the various major automobile manufacturers such as Mercedes-Benz, Suzuki, Honda, Maruti, Tata, Jaguar, Ferrari, etc. The presence of so many automobile manufacturers increases the competition in auto companies and has opened up many choices for the consumers to choose his/her dream vehicle at very competitive rates.

The automobile industry also serves as an important source of employment as jobs are rising in this industry. The automobile industry is growing in all respects and fields. New innovations and new products launch frequently which is a major factor of growth in this sector. There are also various service station networks for the repair and maintenance of your vehicle.

Astonishing fact
Toyota Corolla has held the record of selling 30 million models before being replaced through Toyota Yaris in 2007. This has been one of the most incredible sales rates in the history of Toyota cars.

Future car technologies

Potential future car technologies include new energy sources and materials, which are being developed in order to make automobiles more sustainable, safer, more energy efficient, or less polluting. Cars are being developed in many different ways. With rising gas prices, the future of cars is leaning towards fuel efficiency, energy-savers, hybrid vehicles, battery electric vehicles and fuel-cell vehicles.

Hybrid and electric cars are quite popular for their ability to be plugged into an electric grid and survive on the power of a battery. Several car manufacturers are redesigning their gasoline powered cars to be electric or hybrid-electric.

Hydrogen cars are currently being worked on and, if successful, they could easily be the car of the future. Hydrogen cars can be produced to use sustainable energy resources and water. This hydrogen could be burned in an engine and converted back into electricity by a fuel cell. Essentially it would work like an electric vehicle, being powered on energy.

Other companies are looking at other fuel cells like alcohol fuel, compresses air, garbage, hemp and vegetable oil. Another option for the future is to have electric highways and arterials. There are several cities who have installed electric transportation systems and they are quite successful.

People are attracted to the new 'smart cars'. Smart cars include night-vision imaging system and computers that inform the user of an alternative route if there is a traffic jam. The new technology is making vehicles easier to operate, which maybe quite beneficial with the distractions many drivers face.

The Rolls Royce hood ornament is called the Spirit of Ecstacy.

CARS

There is the concept of the black box technology for cars on the cards. The idea is simple, if airplanes can have them so can cars. Black boxes have proven to be extremely useful in recovering information from airplanes in cases of mishaps. However, its concept is being debated still as it allows the car owners privacy to be compromised. At present general motors' is using them in their newer models and has renamed them to 'recorders' as it stores data on the speed, distance travelled and the visited places. This also helps amongst others, insurance companies who can use the data in case an accident occurs.

Then there's the more interesting feature that allows a car to park for its owners. Cars with such features have been produced already and are being marketed successfully, all the owner has to do is press the brake pedal and the car will carefully avoid all obstacles, make itself parallel and then come to a halt.

Astonishing fact

The Bugatti Veyron's gearbox took 50 engineers and five years to make it perfect.

Lastly and perhaps the most predictable of all car technologies involves cars driving themselves, this is now possible thanks to the recent advances in robotics and GPS technologies. All you will have to do is tell the car where you want to go and the car will take care of the rest. A lot research to perfect this technology is underway and it may not be very long before human drivers become a thing of the past!

After looking at some of these features one can say these are indeed interesting times as cars are evolving with changes in technology and may soon change the very shape of cars as we know them today.

Some famous automobile makers

Some famous automobile makers

Nikolaus August Otto (1832 - 1891)

Nikolaus August Otto was a German engineer who developed the four-stroke internal-combustion engine, which offered the first practical alternative to the steam engine as a power source.

Otto built his first gasoline-powered engine in 1861. In 1876 Otto built an internal-combustion engine utilizing the four-stroke cycle (four strokes of the piston for each explosion). The four-stroke cycle was patented in 1862 by the French engineer Alphonse Beau de Rochas, but since Otto was the first to build an engine based upon this principle, it is commonly known as the **Otto cycle**. Due to its reliability, its efficiency and its relative quietness, Otto's engine was an immediate success.

Gottlieb Daimler (1834 –1900)

Gottlieb Wilhelm Daimler was an engineer, industrial designer and industrialist, born in Germany. He was a pioneer of internal-combustion engines and automobile development.

Daimler and his lifelong business partner Wilhelm Maybach were two inventors whose dream was to create small, high speed engines to be mounted in any kind of locomotion device. They patented in 1885 a precursor of the modern petrol engine which they subsequently fitted to a two-wheeler, considered the first motorcycle and, in the next year to a stagecoach and a boat. They are renowned as the inventors of this **Grandfather Clock** engine.

Later, in 1890, they founded Daimler Motoren Gesellschaft (DMG). They sold their first automobile in 1892. In 1900 Daimler died and Maybach quit DMG in 1907. In 1924, the DMG management signed a long term co-operation agreement with Karl Benz's Benz & Cie., and in 1926 the two companies merged to become Daimler-Benz AG, which is now part of Daimler AG.

Astonishing fact

The paint on a Ferrari F40 is so thin you can see the carbon fibre weave through it. More layers would have added undesirable weight.

CARS

Karl Benz (1844 –1929)

Karl Benz was a German engineer who invented the first automobile with a petroleum driven, internal combustion engine (1885). The engine of that automobile was water-cooled and had electric ignition.

On January 29, 1886, Benz received the first patent (DRP No. 37435) for a gas-fuelled car. It was a three-wheeler; Benz built his first four-wheeled car in 1891. Benz & Company, the company started by the inventor, became the world's largest manufacturer of automobiles by 1900.

At the same time, unknown to Benz, another German, Gottfried Daimler (1834-1900), was also trying to build an automobile. Daimler completed his automobile, the first to have four wheels, in 1886. In 1926 the companies of Benz and Daimler merged to form Daimler-Benz.

Duryea Brothers

America's first gasoline powered commercial car manufacturers were two brothers, Charles Duryea (December 15, 1861 – September 28, 1938) and Frank Duryea ((October 8, 1869 - February 15, 1967). The brothers were bicycle makers who became interested in the new gasoline engines and automobiles.

Charles Duryea and Frank Duryea were the first Americans to build a successful commercial automobile. They were also the first to incorporate an American business for the purpose of building automobiles for sale to the public.

On September 20, 1893, the Duryea brothers' first automobile was constructed and successfully tested on the public streets of Springfield, Massachusetts. Charles Duryea founded the Duryea Motor Wagon Company in 1896, the first company to manufacture and sell gasoline powered vehicles. By 1896, the company had sold thirteen cars of the model Duryea, an expensive limousine, which remained in production into the 1920s.

> ## Astonishing fact
> If a car is hit by lightning, its occupants will generally be safe. The Faraday Effect (discovered by Michael Faraday in 1845) causes the electricity to scatter around the car's metal frame.

Some famous automobile makers

Henry Ford (1863–1947)

Henry Ford created the first inexpensive mass-produced automobile the Model T and revolutionized American industry by developing and refining assembly line manufacturing. Ford began his working life as a machinist, then became an engineer with the Edison Illuminating Company. (He and Thomas Edison remained close friends for decades.) In his spare time Ford tried creating a motorized vehicle, and in 1896 introduced the Quadricycle, a four-wheeled cart with a gasoline engine. In 1903 the Ford Motor Company was founded, and in 1908 Ford introduced the Model T. By 1924 10 million Model T cars had been sold and Detroit had become the auto-making capital of America. Ford remained one of the country's most famous and influential businessmen until his death in 1947.

Louis Renault (1877–1944)

Louis Renault became one of France's most well-known automobile manufacturers, building his first automobile in 1898 and establishing the Renault Motor Company. Renault's numerous patents revolutionized the automotive industry. Chief among his designs were **hydraulic shock absorbers**, the **drum brake** and the **turbocharger**. His hydraulic shock absorber is still a common feature on automobiles today. Renault's other inventions included a transmission that transmitted power and motion from the engine to the wheels through a series of gears without the use of chains or belts.

Renault's first car was called the 'Voiturette,' possessing a three-speed transmission plus a reverse gear. In 1899, Renault and two siblings founded the Renault Brothers Automobile Company and by 1908, Louis Renault had full control of the business.

The first traffic lights were installed in Cleveland, Ohio in 1914.

CARS

Rudolf Diesel (1858 -1913)

In 1892 German engineer Rudolf Diesel patented the engine that bears his name, an internal combustion engine that doesn't require a spark to ignite the fuel-air mixture.

Diesel was born in Paris to German parents and grew up in London, Paris and Munich. In the 1880s he worked as a refrigerator engineer in Munich, but returned to Paris to experiment with engines. In 1892 he won a patent for the diesel engine, but he continued to work on its development for years. The diesel engine allowed trains and ships to operate more efficiently with oil instead of coal, and Diesel quickly became a rich man. In 1913 he vanished overboard from a steamer bound for London; his body washed up ten days later.

Henry Martyn Leland (1843 – 1932)

Henry Martyn Leland is one of the most outstanding figures in automotive history. Best known for developing the Cadillac and the Lincoln, Leland was among the pioneers who set Detroit on its course as

> Porsche is the world's most profitable car manufacturer.

the automobile capital of the world.

Henry Martyn Leland, a former gunmaker and engineer for Ford and Oldsmobile, founded Cadillac in 1902. Specializing in precise craftsmanship and using standardized parts, Leland built a four-cylinder Cadillac 30 in 1909 and made his company successful enough that it was purchased by General Motors soon after. In 1915, Cadillac's powerful, smooth and reliable straight-eight engines set the standard for large ultra-luxury cars. Despite some periods of uncertainty, revisions and technical innovations over the years have ensured Cadillac's popularity and reputation as a luxury marque to this day.

Some famous cars

Aston Martin DB5

The Aston Martin DB5 is a luxury sports car that was made by Aston Martin. Released in 1963, it was an evolution of the final series of DB4. The DB series was named honouring David Brown (the head of Aston Martin from 1947–1972).

The DB5 is famous for being the first and most recognised James Bond car. It has been featured in several films, most notably Goldfinger, Thunderball, GoldenEye, Tomorrow Never Dies and Casino Royale.

Regarded by many as the most beautiful Aston Martin produced, DB5 shares many similar traits to the DB4. Aston had considered the DB4 a success, but the DB5 sold twice as fast, with 1021 cars being built during its brief two-year production.

> It's a popularly-cited myth that F1 cars can drive upside down! They can't.

Bugatti Veyron

The Bugatti Veyron 16.4 is the most powerful, most expensive and fastest street-legal production car in the world, with a proven top speed of over 400 km/h (407 km/h or 253 mph). The car is built by Volkswagen AG subsidiary Bugatti Automobiles SAS and is sold under the legendary Bugatti marque. It is named after racing driver Pierre Veyron, who won the 24 hours of Le Mans in 1939 while racing for the original Bugatti firm. The Veyron features a W16 engine—16 cylinders in 4 banks of 4 cylinders.

According to Volkswagen, the final production Veyron engine produces between 1020 and 1040 metric hp (1006 to 1026 SAE net hp); so it makes the Veyron the most powerful production road-car engine in history.

CARS

Rolls-Royce Phantom

The Rolls-Royce Phantom is a luxury saloon automobile made by Rolls-Royce Motor Cars, a BMW subsidiary. It was launched in 2003 and is the first Rolls-Royce model made under the ownership of BMW. It has a 6.8 L, 48-valve, V12 engine that produces 453 hp (338 kW) and 531 ft·lbf (720 N·m) of torque. The engine is derived from BMW's existing V12 power plant. It is 1.63 m (63 in) tall, 1.99 m (74.8 in) wide, 5.83 m (228 in) long, and weighs 2485 kg (5478 lb). The body of the car is built on an aluminium space frame and the Phantom can accelerate to 60 mph (100 km/h) in 5.7 seconds.

Astonishing fact

The F1 race cars can go from 0 to 160 km/h speed and then back to 0 speeds in just 4 seconds!

Ferrari Enzo

The Ferrari Enzo, named after the Ferrari's owner, is a high performance sports car which is well noted for its styling features. The price of the Ferari Enzo is currently estimated at over $1,000,000.

The body of the Ferarri Enzo is made of carbon fibre; as a result, the car is of less weight. The car features aerodynamic (study of how air resistance affects an object) subsystems for better safety and performance. Vehicles with an aerodynamic design tend to be more stable at higher speeds.

The Ferrari Enzo reaches the speed of 97km/h in 3.4 seconds and the top speed is about 349km/h. The Ferrari Enzo features 6-speed Semi-Automatic transmission and the gear shifts can be performed easily and smoothly even at higher loads. The wheels are wrapped with Bridgestone tires and it features carbon ceramic discs with six piston callipers. The car also features Anti Braking System and power steering.

Some famous cars

Leblanc Mirabeau

The 2009 LeBlanc Mirabeau is a high performance race car. It was specially designed to feature at the 24 Hours Le Mans race. The car delivers high performance, smooth driving and it can be driven on normal roads as well.

The top speed of the LeBlanc Mirabeau is about 370km/h and the price of the car is about $748,140.

For those in tune with true performance, it goes without saying that the Leblanc Mirabeau is not just a car. In fact, it is really more than a supercar. It is a true race car. The fact that it was designed for the streets just makes it that much more of a dream to serious vehicle enthusiasts everywhere.

Maybach Landaulet

The new Maybach Landaulet resurrects the legend of the classic luxury landaulets, a feature of which is that only the chauffeur's area is closed. An extra-large folding roof opens up over the rear-seat passengers when required, leaving no obstructions between them and the blue sky above.

> Electric door locks where first introduced in 1956, later in 1958 the first remote adjusted side view mirrors was introduced.

When closed, the black soft-top of the Maybach Landaulet rests on the roof frame and is wind and weather-proof. The passenger compartment in the spacious rear of the vehicle is styled a tasteful white, whereas the chauffeur's area is entirely in black. Though this does make the respective roles quite clear, the seat behind the steering wheel of the Maybach Landaulet should certainly be one of the most coveted workplaces for a chauffeur. For here, too, only exceptionally high-grade materials are used. The Maybach Landaulet cost EUR 900,000 (or US$ 1.35 million).

CARS

Lamborghini Reventón

A super car without equals, the Lamborghini Reventón is a road vehicle with an extreme specification. It has a coherent style, angular with sharp lines, inspired by the very latest aeronautics.

Its production is limited to 20 models and it was sold out before the cars were even made. The cost of owning the Lamburghini Reventon is 1,000,000 Euros (1.6 million dollars). It has the most powerful Lamborghini engine and it is the fastest Lamborghini out there. It has a powerful 640 bhp V12 engine which enables it to accelerate from 0 to 97km/h in 3.3 seconds and reach a top speed of 339km/h.

Porsche Carrera GT

Any car can take you from one place to another. But not many can go from zero to 97 km/hr in just over three seconds or hit a top speed of 330 km/hr! And not many cars feel as at home on the racetrack as they do on the roadway. The V10, 605-horsepower Porsche Carrera GT achieves all of the above.

The Carrera GT is among a rare breed of supercars — exotic, high-performance automobiles that are built for ultimate speed and handling on the road. Its ultra-lightweight, high-tech design places the Carrera GT among the top of its class.

> The law on emission control was first introduced in California in 1965. After that many safety devices also became mandatory in vehicles.

Test Your MEMORY

1. What is a car?

2. Write briefly about the history of cars.

3. Name the countries which produce the most cars.

4. Write briefly about the parts of a car.

5. What are the advantages of cars?

6. Write about the disadvantages of cars.

7. Write briefly about the cost and maintenance of cars.

8. Write briefly about the automobile industry.

9. What are the future car technologies?

10. Write briefly about two famous automobile makers.

11. Write briefly about two famous cars.

12. Which is the most expensive car in the world?

CARS

Index

A

Amedee Bollee 4
Aston Martin DB5 27
automobile 3, 4, 5, 6, 8, 10, 14, 15, 20, 23, 24, 25, 26, 28

B

battery 10, 12, 18, 21
brakes 10, 16, 19
Bugatti Veyron 22, 27

C

Cannstatt-Daimler 6
car 3, 4, 5, 6, 7, 8, 9, 10, 11, 12, 13, 14, 16, 17, 18, 19, 21, 22, 24, 25, 26, 27, 28, 29, 30
Charles Edgar Duryea 6
chassis 6, 11
Curved Dash Oldsmobile 5, 8

D

dashboard instruments 11
diesel 3, 26
driveline 9
Duryea Motor Wagon Company 7, 24

E

electrical system 10, 18
engine 4, 5, 6, 7, 8, 9, 10, 11, 12, 16, 17, 18, 19, 21, 23, 24, 25, 26, 27, 28, 30

F

Fardier 4
Ferrari Enzo 28
frame 11, 24, 28, 29
Francois Isaac de Rivaz 4
Frank Duryea 6, 7, 24
fuel gauge 11

G

gasoline 3, 5, 6, 7, 8, 9, 21, 23, 24, 25
George Baldwin Selden 6
Gottlieb Wilhelm Daimler 23

H

Henry Ford 5, 8, 25
Henry Martyn Leland 26

J

Jean Joseph Etienne Lenoir 5

K

Karl Benz 5, 23, 24

L

Leblanc Mirabeau 29
Louis Renault 25

M

Maybach Landaulet 29
Model T 5, 8, 25
muffler 12

N

Nicolas Joseph Cugnot 4

Nikolaus August Otto 23

O

oil pressure gauge 11
Otto cycle 23

P

patents 3, 7, 25
petrol 3, 23
pollution 15
Porsche Carrera GT 30

Q

quadricycle 8, 25

R

radiator 12
Ransom E. Olds 5
Robert Anderson 6
Rolls-Royce Phantom 28
Rudolf Diesel 26

S

speedometer 11
steering system 11
suspension system 11

T

tachometer 11
tires 10, 28

W

wheels 3, 9, 10, 11, 12, 17, 24, 25, 28
Wilhelm Maybach 5, 6, 23

PEGASUS ENCYCLOPEDIA LIBRARY

Transport
LAND TRANSPORT

Edited by: Pallabi B. Tomar
Managing editor: Tapasi De
Designed by: Vijesh Chahal, Anil Kumar and Rohit Kumar
Illustrated by: Suman S. Roy, Tanoy Choudhury
Colouring done by: Vinay Kumar, Sonu, Kiran Kumari & Pradeep Kumar

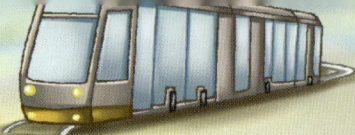

CONTENTS

What is land transport? 3

History of land transport 4

Categories of land transportation 7

Types of land transport vehicles 8

Roads and highways 12

Traffic control 14

Advantages of road transport 16

Disadvantages 17

Land transport and environment 18

Some famous land transportation vehicles 21

Test Your Memory 31

Index 32

What is land transport?

Land transport includes vehicles which neither sail on the oceans nor fly in the air. This means land transport consists of cars, vans, buses, two-wheelers, trains and a couple of other vehicles which travel on the roads. Bicycles also fall into this transport category.

But land transport did not impact the environment and climate until the invention of the engine driven vehicles. When people began to make use of fossil fuels in order to run these vehicles, and in the process increased pollution, scientists began to find ways to make land transport more environment friendly. The amount of these vehicles has been virtually exploding in the last century and is still growing, particularly in the developing countries.

This is the main form of transportation in the world today. People move about land with the help of their own power, use domestic animals or use a combination of the wheel with electric or fuel powered engines to move people and freight quickly and efficiently.

Astonishing fact

An average new car today consumes 15 per cent less fuel per 100 km than 10 years ago.

LAND TRANSPORT

History of land transport

Land transportation first began with the carrying of goods by people. The ancient civilizations of Central America, Mexico and Peru transported materials in that fashion over long roads and bridges.

The first road vehicles were two-wheeled carts, with crude disks fashioned from stone serving as the wheels. Used by the Sumerians (c.3000 B.C.), such simple wagons were precursors of the chariot, which the Egyptians and Greeks, among others, developed from a lumbering cart into a work of beauty. Under the Chou dynasty (c.1000 B.C.), the Chinese constructed the world's first permanent road system. The Romans built 85,000 km of roads, primarily for military reasons, throughout their vast empire. The most famous of these was the Appian Way which begun in 325 B.C.

Four-wheeled carriages were developed towards the end of the 12th century; they transported only the privileged until the late 18th century, when Paris licensed **omnibuses** and **stagecoaches** began to operate in England. In the United States the demands of an ever-extending frontier led to the creation of the **Conestoga wagon** and the **prairie schooner**, so that goods and families could be transported across the eastern mountains, the Great Plains, and westward.

The great period of railroad building in the second half of the 19th century made earlier methods of transportation largely obsolete within the United States. After World War I, however, automobiles, buses, and trucks came to exceed the railroads in importance.

> The first bus, known as a carrosse, was introduced in Paris by Blaise Pascal, in 1662. It was horse-drawn and carried eight people. Carosses was a great innovation, as it ran every few minutes.

History of land transport

Compared to transport by boats and ships, transportation on land was slower, more uncomfortable and more dangerous. Goods were transported on rivers and on the seas, rather than over land. Nevertheless, the Roman Empire had an excellent system of roads. The army built most of the roads because they allowed soldiers to travel quickly in wartime and formed a basis for the administration of the Empire. Some of the old roads are still used today. However, the roads made it also easier for the merchants to transport goods around the Roman Empire.

The actual means of transportation were provided by horses, donkeys, animal-pulled vehicles and of course by foot. Horses had problems with the metalled road surfaces and wore hippo sandals to protect their feet. These objects have been found in small numbers.

The earliest forms of road transport were horses or oxen, which carried goods over dirt tracks. Military officers travelled on the back of a horse and the army had stations at which an officer or courier could exchange a tired horse for a fresh one.

Most of the time, the traders also went on foot or used a donkey or horse to ride on it. They put the goods into bags, which hung at the sides of the donkey, because they couldn't afford wooden carts. For the transport of heavier and bigger amounts of goods the Romans used wagons, made out of wood, pulled by horses or oxen. As the roads were paved with hard-wearing stone slabs, transport was not very comfortable either for the animal or for the merchant.

> **Coventry Machine Company made the first all-metal bicycle called Ariel in 1870. It was the first machine to have wheels with wire spokes.**

LAND TRANSPORT

The wagons, which were used for transporting goods, had either 2 or 4 wheels. These wheels may have been simple wooden disks or had 8, sometimes even up to 12 spokes. They were banded with iron. The heavier carts, made out of oak wood, were pulled by oxen and the lighter ones by horses or mules. The plaustrum was one of the earliest and simplest four-wheel vehicles found in Rome. It was just a flat board on wheels.

When a number of people needed to travel together or when goods or luggage had to be carried, a four-wheeled wagon called raeda was used. As the Romans did not have harness (the combination of straps, bands, etc. by which a horse is fastened to its loads) suitable for horses, usually heavy wagons were pulled by oxen or mules. The lightest vehicles in general use were two-wheeled carts with a pair of seats perched high up.

The Romans used also various other kinds of vehicles and modes of transport, for instance the lectica, a framework of canvas stretched between two parallel bars, which was similar to an 18th century sedan chair, an enclosed vehicle for one person. This 'portable couch' was used only for rich people and it was carried by slaves.

> Etienne Lenoir, a Belgian enameller turned engineer who lived in Paris, invented the first motor car in 1862.

Lectica

Plaustrum

Categories of land transportation

Eduard Delamare-Deboutteville, of Fontaine-le-Bourg, France, made the first petrol-engined car in 1883.

Transport on roads can be roughly grouped into two categories—transportation of goods and transportation of people. In many countries licensing requirements and safety regulations ensure a separation of the two industries.

The nature of road transportation of goods depends, apart from the degree of development of the local infrastructure, on the distance the goods are transported by road, the weight and volume of the individual shipment and the type of goods transported. For short distances and light, small shipments a van or pickup truck maybe used. For large shipments even if less than a full truckload a truck is more appropriate. In some countries cargo is transported by road in horse-drawn carriages, donkey carts or other non-motorized mode. Delivery services are sometimes considered a separate category from cargo transport. In many places fast food is transported on roads by various types of vehicles. People are transported on roads either in individual cars or automobiles or public transports like bus, trains, etc. Special modes of individual transport by road like rickshaws or velotaxis may also be locally available.

LAND TRANSPORT

Types of land transport vehicles

Ground transport was present during prehistoric times first from simple sledges that were made from multiple pieces of tree branches tied together to later the creation of two-wheeled carts made from stone that were shaped to a disc to form the wheels. It wasn't until the 12th century that the first four-wheeled horse drawn carriage was created to transport the rich and the privileged.

It was much later during the 18th century where omnibuses and stagecoaches were employed in England, Paris and other various parts of Europe. The United States soon followed pursuit utilizing what was known as the **prairie schooner** and **Conestoga wagon**. These not only allowed them to transport goods and people over flat land but also through rough terrains and mountain areas. With the continuous growth in need for transportation of goods and people, the railway system soon took over in the United States, providing connections to most major cities and isolated country sites and farms. However, it was until after World War I, that car, buses, trucks came into use and exceeded the importance of railroads services.

> Karl Benz of Mannheim, Germany, made the first successful petrol-engined car in 1885. It was driven for the first time in 1886 at a little over nine miles an hour.

Today, the world's ground transportation is like a web that can take you or any goods to any destination at any time. Each country has its own transport infrastructure and network that delivers the needs to its population. The basic land transport network usually includes the following:

1. **Automobiles**
   - Car
   - Taxi
   - Bus
2. **Railway System**
   - Train
   - Tram
3. **Other Ground Transportation**
   - Motorcycle
   - Bicycle

Types of land transport vehicles

Car

Cars are also commonly known as motor cars and automobiles. They are wheeled vehicles.

It is either powered by fuel such as petrol, diesel, LPG, etc. The act of operating the vehicle is called driving. In a vehicle, there is a seat for the driver and two or more passenger seats.

Taxi

Taxi is a form of public transport on the ground where a driver picks up a passenger or several passengers who wish to travel to the same destination upon request.

Fee is charge as per kilometre or location. Although, taxi is a form of public transport, but at any one given time the driver will be only taking one or a group of passengers who will be going to the same destination.

Bus

The word 'bus' arises from the Latin word omnibus meaning 'for all'. Omnibuses were first used in 1662 in Paris, France and at that time they were drawn by horses.

In the early 20th century motorized buses powered by gasoline or diesel came into use, and it was able to take passengers to places where trains could not reach. Today, buses are one of the most common forms of public transport used in most major cities around the world. It is used to take commuters to work, home and shopping. It is used as a school bus, tour bus, etc.

> Gottlieb Daimler of Cannstatt, Germany, produced the first four-wheeled car at the same time as Karl Benz, also driven in 1886. Since then, both firms continued to develop various cars until the consolidation of Daimler-Benz in 1926.

LAND TRANSPORT

> Gottlieb Daimler built the first motor cycle in 1885. It was ridden by his son, Paul, for six miles.

Train

Another commonly used land transport around the world is trains. It can consist of a single or multiple connected rail vehicles which are interconnected and move together along a railway system. Trains can transport passengers travelling between stations where distance can vary from under 1 km to much more. It is also used as freight trains to carry goods in bulk over long distances. Transporting goods via freight trains is highly economical and energy efficient when transporting long distances.

There are many other special kinds of trains that run on special 'railways'. They are **atmospheric railways**, **monorails** (single rail trains), high-speed railways (**bullet trains** seen in Japan), maglev, **rubber-tired underground, funicular** and **cog railways**.

Tram

The tram is also known as the tramcar, trolley and streetcar which travels wholly or partly along a form of railway system or tracks laid on city streets. They are designed to transport passengers within close range villages, towns and cities. It is only on rare occasion that they are used as freight to transport goods.

Almost all passenger trams are propelled by an electric motor which is fed from an overhead line especially designed to run on tracks set up on public roads. Due to road developments and the increased use of private vehicles on roads, the use of trams as a form of transport has decreased dramatically.

Motorcycle

A motorcycle is a two-wheeled motor vehicle resembling a heavy bicycle, sometimes having two saddles and a sidecar with a third wheel. There are many different types of motorcycles. These can include standard bikes, road motorcycles, cruiser, sport bikes, touring and sport bikes, scooters, mopeds and much more. The first motor tricycle was built in 1884 in England, and the first gasoline-engine motorcycle was built by Gottlieb Daimler in 1885. Motorcycles were widely used after 1910, especially by the armed forces in World War I. After 1950 a larger, heavier motorcycle was used mainly for touring and sport competitions. The moped, a light, low-speed motor bicycle that can also be pedalled, was developed mainly in Europe, and the sturdier Italian-made motor scooter also became popular for its economy.

Bicycle

Bicycles are also commonly called a bike. It is a light-framed two-wheeled vehicle that is driven by the movement of constant pedalling of a pedal by a person. All bicycles are fitted with pneumatic tyres, with the rear wheel being propelled by the rider through a crank, chain and gear mechanism.

Bicycles are becoming more and more popular because it is environmentally friendly as it does not turn out any toxic gases in to the air. It is also a great way to exercise.

Hildebrand Wolfmuller, of Munich, Germany, manufactured the first motor cycle for sale to the public in 1894, the same year that Aleandre Darracq of France, began to manufacture them too.

Roads and highways

In many countries, roads and highways provide the dominant mode of land transportation. They form the backbone of the economy, often carrying more than 80 per cent of passengers and over 50 per cent of freight in a country, and providing essential links to vast rural road networks.

Highways are the most important part of the automobile industry. If there were no roads or highways there would be no need for automobiles. Highways allow drivers to get from destination to destination within cities and states. Highways can be large or small in the number of lanes available in each direction. There are different highway designs across the world. Highways can consist of tunnels, bridges and even ferries.

Of the various modes of transport that connect the cities and villages of the country, road transport constitutes the crucial link. Road infrastructure facilitates movement of men and material, helps trade and commerce, links industry and agriculture to markets and opens up backward regions. In addition, the road system also provides last-mile (final leg of the journey) connection for other modes of transport such as railways, airports, ports and inland waterway transport and complements the efforts of these modes in meeting the needs of transportation.

Trams reduce congestion in city centres by providing people with a quick, reliable, high-quality alternative to the car. They can reduce road traffic by up to 14 per cent.

Roads and highways

Roads are the vital lifelines of the economy making possible trade and commerce. Roads are the most preferred modes of transportation and considered as one of the cost effective modes of transportation. Roads are easily accessible to each individual. Roads facilitate movement of both men and materials anywhere within a country. It helps in socio-economic development as well as brings national integration. An efficient and well-established network of roads is desired for promoting trade and commerce in any country and also fulfils the needs of a sound transportation system for sustained economic development.

Roads are among the most important public assets in many countries. Improvements of roads bring immediate and sometimes dramatic benefits to communities through better access to hospitals, schools and markets; greater comfort, speed, and safety; and lower vehicle operating costs.

For these benefits to be sustained, however, road improvements must be followed by well-planned programs of road maintenance. Without regular maintenance, roads can rapidly fall into disrepair, preventing communities from reaping the longer term benefits of road improvement such as increased agricultural production and an increase in school enrolment.

Although the need for maintenance is widely recognized, it is still not adequately implemented in many countries. Many countries spend just 20–50 per cent of what they should be spending on maintenance of their road network.

LAND TRANSPORT

Traffic control

Nearly all roadways are built with devices meant to control traffic. Most notable to the motorist are those meant to communicate directly with the driver. Broadly, these fall into three categories—signs, signals or pavement markings. They help the driver navigate, assign the right-of-way at intersections, indicate laws such as speed limits and parking regulations, advise of potential hazards, indicate passing and no passing zones and assures traffic is orderly and safe.

200 years ago these devices were signs, nearly all informal. In the late 19th century signals began to appear in the biggest cities at a few highly congested intersections. They were manually operated, and consisted of semaphores, flags or paddles, or in some cases coloured electric lights, all modelled on railroad signals. In the 20th century signals were automated, at first with electromechanical devices and later with computers. Signals can be quite sophisticated with vehicle sensors embedded in the pavement, the signal can control and choreograph the turning movements of heavy traffic in the most complex of intersections. In the 1920s traffic engineers learned how to coordinate signals along a thoroughfare to increase its speeds and volumes. In the 1980s, with computers, similar coordination of whole networks became possible.

Traffic is the business of moving people and cargo from one place to another. Farmers have to transfer their products from their farms to the market and this involves a lot of movement. Goods are also in need of transporting from the manufacturing plants to the stores, etc. There's a need to manage the movement of individuals and goods in a safe and efficient manner. We must understand that effective transportation of goods from place to place gets rid of cost and, consequently, keeps the costs of goods down. Good traffic control management likewise helps lower the probability of accidents occurring.

Traffic control

All means of transportation require productive traffic control. In air traffic control, the management has to be very effective in order to avoid the collision of airplanes that are taking off and making landings. Clearance has to be provided by the air traffic controller alone as they monitor the number of airplanes that are supposed to arrive at a particular scheduled time. Doing this, the traffic controllers can guide the airplane traffic safely and efficiently.

In road traffic, traffic lights can be very helpful to manage traffic at intersections. The colours of these traffic lights guide the drivers on when to stop or when to go thereby preventing cars from colliding. A separate lane for automobiles turning left or right can be provided with a lighted arrow to minimize interference with opposing traffic. A separate lane can be provided with a lighted green arrow permitting the autos to turn left without opposing traffic.

The most common road accidents occur when drivers do not obey the traffic lights. Drivers endanger themselves and other people whenever they don't follow the traffic lights. Statistics show that reckless driving causes more accidents and injuries to individuals and pedestrians than when drivers drive defensively and safely.

Traffic control also involves traffic rules and laws to be followed. Strict execution of these laws and rules will efficiently regulate the smooth and orderly flow of traffic on the road. Traffic control is the organization of numerous rules, traffic signals or signs, marked lanes, intersections and junctions. Some may have thorough or complex road rules while others will rely more on the driver's good sense in safe driving.

Good traffic control management is also essential in construction zones, road repairs, functions and events, and road disruptions caused by accidents. Efficient control is very important as a way to effectively handle the flow of automobiles and pedestrians in these situations.

LAND TRANSPORT

Advantages of road transport

Road transport has the following advantages:-

- It is a relatively cheaper mode of transport as compared to the other modes.

- Perishable goods can be transported at a faster speed by road carriers over a short distance.

- It is a flexible mode of transport as loading and unloading is possible at any destination. It provides door-to-door service.

- It helps people to travel and carry goods from one place to another, in places which are not connected by other means of transport like hilly areas.

- It is reliable as goods are under direct control of the drivers.

- It is relatively safe for goods since there is little handling.

Disadvantages

It has the following limitations:-

- Due to limited carrying capacity, road transport is not economical for long distance transportation of goods.
- Transportation of heavy goods or goods in bulk by road involves high cost.
- It is affected by adverse weather conditions. Floods, rain, landslide, etc., sometimes create obstructions to land transport.
- It is a slower mode of transportation.
- Land transport burns more of our already diminishing fossil fuels.
- There is also a higher risk of accident.

Land transport and environment

The issue of land transport and the environment is paradoxical in nature. From one side, land transport increases the mobility demands of passengers and freight. This takes into consideration both local and international trade. On the other side, transport activities have resulted in growing levels of motorization and congestion. As a result, the land transport sector is becoming increasingly linked to environmental problems. With a technology relying heavily on the combustion of hydrocarbons, notably with the internal combustion engine, the impacts of land transport over environmental systems has increased with motorization. This has reached a point where transportation activities are a dominant factor behind the emission of most pollutants and thus affecting the environment.

The impact of land transport on the environment is a subject of growing concern. Roads and traffic are variously condemned for increasing the noise levels, poor childhood respiratory health, loss of wildlife habitat, the division and dislocation of communities and many other manifestations of social and environmental pathology.

Land transport also affects water quality because oil and particles from vehicles get washed into creeks and rivers. In urban environments, run-off from roads goes into storm water drains. These feed into creeks and rivers, which eventually meet the sea.

Oil is a particularly harmful water pollutant. Even a small amount of oil can severely contaminate waterways. Oil can be toxic to aquatic life and smother plants and animals.

Particles from the wear of tyres, brakes and other components get washed into the storm water and pollute waterways.

When it rains, air pollution from cars mixes with rainwater and falls to the ground, adding to water pollution.

Detergents also contaminate waterways.

Cars produce greenhouse gases that contribute to global warming and climate change. The main greenhouse gas is carbon dioxide. Others include nitrous oxide and methane.

Greenhouse gases occur naturally in the atmosphere, trapping some of the heat radiated from the Earth's surface. Increases in the amount of these gases, mainly through the burning of carbon-based fuels such as coal and oil, are increasing the average temperature of the Earth, affecting local climates including temperature and rainfall.

Air pollution has negative health effects, especially for vulnerable people, including those with allergic and respiratory conditions, such as asthma, hay fever and sinusitis, and respiratory and lung conditions commonly associated with the elderly. Research suggests that certain air pollutants (e.g. benzene) are carcinogenic.

LAND TRANSPORT

Vehicle exhaust emissions are a major source of air pollution in some areas, particularly around busy road corridors. Pollutants include carbon monoxide (CO), nitrogen dioxide (NO2), benzene and particulate matter.

Heavy metals and petroleum products from vehicles can contaminate both land and water. Land transport is also responsible for some of the extensive heavy metal contamination of some harbours and estuarine areas. Contaminated water can make water unsafe to swim in or drink. Culverts for transport infrastructure can disrupt fish migration. Suspended sediments from road works for example, can affect water clarity, favouring species that prefer cloudy conditions.

Noise and vibrations can affect people who live or work near busy roads or rail facilities. This can cause stress, exacerbate existing medical conditions and interfere with daily activities such as communicating or sleeping. High levels of noise can also bring down property values.

Some famous land transportation vehicles

Bugatti Veyron

The Bugatti Veyron 16.4 is the most powerful, most expensive and fastest street-legal production car in the world, with a proven top speed of over 407 km/h. The car is built by Volkswagen AG subsidiary Bugatti Automobiles SAS and is sold under the legendary Bugatti marque. It is named after racing driver Pierre Veyron, who won the 24 hours of Le Mans in 1939 while racing for the original Bugatti firm. The Veyron features a W16 engine—16 cylinders in 4 banks of 4 cylinders.

According to Volkswagen, the final production Veyron engine produces between 1020 and 1040 metric hp (1006 to 1026 SAE net hp), so it makes the Veyron the most powerful production road-car engine in history.

The $1.3 million Veyron will reach a top speed of 407 km/h; a speed it can maintain for 12 minutes before all the fuel is gone. The car can hit 96 km/h in just 2.5 seconds, 160 km/h in 5.5 seconds, and 241 km/h in 9.8 seconds. Getting to 322 km/h takes 18.3 seconds and 402 km/h takes 42.3 seconds.

A special key is required to unlock the Veyron's top speed of 407 km/h. The car is then lowered to just 3.5 inches from the ground. A hydraulic spoiler extends at speed, and it can also serve as an air brake.

LAND TRANSPORT

Rolls-Royce Phantom

The Rolls-Royce Phantom is a luxury saloon automobile made by Rolls-Royce Motor Cars, a BMW subsidiary. It was launched in 2003 and is the first Rolls-Royce model made under the ownership of BMW. It has a 6.8 L, 48-valve, V12 engine that produces 453 hp (338 kW) and 531 ft·lbf (720 N·m) of torque. The engine is derived from BMW's existing V12 power plant. It is 1.63 m (63 in) tall, 1.99 m (74.8 in) wide, 5.83 m (228 in) long, and weighs 2485 kg (5478 lb). The body of the car is built on an aluminium space frame and the Phantom can accelerate to 100 km/h (60 mph) in 5.7 seconds.

The Rolls Royce Phantom is a premium ultra luxury sedan offered in extended and regular wheelbase model that provides comfortable seating capacity for five passengers. Most expected standard features include cast aluminium 21 inch wheels, Lexicon Logic 7 15-speaker surround sound system with satellite radio with lifetime subscription, single-CD in dash player, auxiliary audio jack and glove box mounted six-CD changer, adjustable air suspension, multifunction electronics controller, rear and front parking sensors, Rolls-Royce Assist emergency telematics, power-closing rear coach doors, voice command functionality, power closing trunk lid, power front soft close doors, navigation system, sunroof, keyless ignition, multizone climate control, Bluetooth, heated rear and front seats, veneered picnic tables built in rear seatbacks, driver memory functions, leather headliner with cashmere and wool accent panels and power telescoping and tilt steering column.

Some famous land transportation vehicles

Tata Trucks

Tata trucks are amongst the most sought-after heavy commercial vehicles (HCV) in India. Tata Motors is the fourth largest truck manufacturer in the world. Established in 1945, it first rolled out its vehicle in 1954. Since then, more than 4 million Tata vehicles run on Indian roads. It has its manufacturing units located in various locations across the country including Jamshedpur, Pantnagar, Pune, Dharwad and Lucknow.

Tata trucks have created a niche in the truck industry worldwide. Tata trucks also lead in the key medium and heavy truck category with an index of 90 in the segment of Tractor-Trailer.

Volvo Trucks

Volvo is the second largest producer of heavy duty trucks in the world. There are few countries you can visit where there isn't a Volvo truck on the road.

Based in Sweden, Volvo trucks is a truck manufacturer owned by the Volvo Group. The company currently employs over 22,000 people around the world and has its global headquarters in Gothenburg.

Volvo trucks produce and sell over 100,000 trucks each year. Approximately 95 per cent of the trucks they produce are in the heavy weight class above 16 tons. A large proportion of Volvo trucks are manufactured in the USA along with Sweden, Brazil and Belgium.

Volvo trucks are renowned for their safety record and are considered to be some of the safest vehicles in the world. They are also incredibly reliable and durable.

LAND TRANSPORT

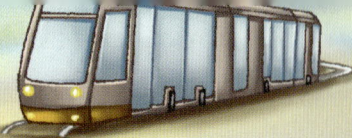

Trans-Siberian Express

The Trans Siberian Express travels 9,297 km between Moscow and Vladivostok. The line opened in 1914 and is the world's longest continuous rail line.

The **Trans-Siberian Railway** or Transsib is the name given to the three rail routes that traverse Siberia from Moscow.

- The **Trans-Mongolian** goes from Moscow to Beijing, China via Ulaanbaatar, Mongolia.
- The **Trans-Manchurian** travels through Siberia and Chinese Manchuria to Beijing.
- The **Trans-Siberian** proper goes from Moscow to the Pacific terminus of Vladivostok.

The Trans-Siberian Railway is the longest railway in the world. It was built between 1891 and 1916 to connect Moscow with the Far-East city of Vladivostok. En route it passes through the cities of Perm, Yekaterinburg, Omsk, Novosibirsk, Krasnoyarsk, Irkutsk, Chita and Khabarovsk.

Eurostar

The Eurostar service was launched on November 14, 1994, to carry passengers between London, Paris and Brussels through the channel tunnel. It can reach speeds of 300 km/h. In its first ten years it carried a total of 59 million passengers.

Eurostar is a train service that connects London with Paris and Brussels. Trains cross the English Channel through the Channel Tunnel. In addition to the three destination cities, some Eurostar services currently stop en route at Ashford in Kent and Lille in northern France. Eurostar, which began services in November 1994, is a joint venture between Belgian, French and British railway companies.

The Eurostar service has established a dominant share of the market for travellers on the routes it serves – 68 per cent for London-Paris and 63 per cent for London-Brussels as of November 2004.

LAND TRANSPORT

Shinkansen (Bullet trains)

Due to its dense population, Japan dumped its focus on cars and concentrated on shinkansen (Bullet trains), the world fastest scheduled rail services. They were introduced in 1964 to coincide with the Tokyo Olympic Games.

Japan's main islands of Honshu and Kyushu are served by a network of high speed train lines that connect Tokyo with most of the country's major cities. Japan's high speed trains (Bullet trains) are called shinkansen and are operated by Japan Railways (JR).

Running at speeds of up to 300 km/h, the shinkansen is known for punctuality (most trains depart on time to the second), comfort (relatively silent cars with spacious, always forward facing seats), safety (no fatal accidents in its history) and efficiency. Thanks to the Japan Rail Pass, the shinkansen can also be a very cost effective means of travel.

The shinkansen network consists of multiple lines, among which the Tokaido Shinkansen (Tokyo - Nagoya - Kyoto - Osaka) is the oldest and the most popular. All shinkansen lines (except the Akita and Yamagata Shinkansen) run on tracks that are exclusively built for and used by shinkansen trains. Most lines are served by multiple train categories, ranging from the fastest category that stops only at major stations to the slowest category that stops at every station along the way.

Some famous land transportation vehicles

Blue Train

This is one of the world's most luxurious trains and it has operated between Cape Town and Tshwane (Pretoria), South Africa since 1939. The train, carriages and decor are mainly blue – hence the name.

It's the most famous train in South Africa, and one of the most famous trains in the world. South Africa's 'Blue Train' links Cape Town with Pretoria once or twice a week, year round. With a one-way fare of about £890 or $1,300 per person for two people travelling together even in the low season, it's now aimed squarely at foreign visitors. Single passengers cannot opt to share, so should reckon on paying £1,330 or $2,030 one-way for sole use of a 2-berth compartment. However, The Blue Train is definitely the most luxurious way to travel between these two cities.

The Blue Train offers two types of room— 'Deluxe' compartments have either a double bed or two single beds and en suite shower or small bath. 'Luxury' compartments cost a bit more and are almost identical, but have a full size bath and a video. The train has a dining car and two lounge cars (one smoking, one non-smoking) and one of the two train sets has an observation car at the rear, allowing you to look back along the line.

LAND TRANSPORT

Harley-Davidson Motorcycle

Known as the motorcycle of motorcycles, Harley Davidson Motorcycles remains constant throughout the ages with its varying style and fashions. Harley-Davidson began in 1901 with William

S. Harley and childhood friend Arthur Davidson starting work on a motor-bicycle, with the first motorcycles available to purchase in 1905. The growth of the company included supplying around 15,000 machines to the military forces during World War I, and by 1920, Harley-Davidson was the largest motorcycle manufacturer in the world. In 1929, the flathead engine was introduced, followed by the Knucklehead in 1941. By the outbreak of World War II, only two American motorcycle companies existed, with Harley-Davidson producing over 90,000 military vehicles, and after the war ended, many of these then came back into civilian hands at relatively low prices.

The company produces traditional cruiser motorcycles with V-Twin engines. Popular models of Harley Davidson include the Sportster, Road King, Electra Glide, Dyna Glide and Softail.

The Harley Bikes are ideal for fast rides on the highway. The unique design and the configuration symbolize adventure and wilderness. The engine power starts from 750 cc. This chopper bike is usually meant for sports biking.

Some famous land transportation vehicles

Suzuki Hayabusa

Suzuki Hayabusa is among the most popular sports motorcycles ever produced. Since its inception it is widely regarded as the fastest bike in production in the world. The bike is also known as GSX1300R in some countries. In the unrestricted environment of a racetrack, Hayabusa can thrill anyone with its awesome power.

The Hayabusa's 4-stroke, four-cylinder liquid-cooled 1299cc engine enables it to produce massive peak power of 175 bhp at 9800 rpm and reach from 0-100 km/h in three seconds flat!

Hayabusa was introduced by Suzuki in 1999. It derived its name from the Japanese term for the Peregrine Falcon, the fastest creature on the planet with speed exceeding 300 km/h. Hayabusa was a massive success right from its inception, encouraging other bike manufacturers to come up with similar speedsters. However, none of its competitors was as successful in the US and European markets. The 2008 model carried a MSRP of US$11,999.

LAND TRANSPORT

Kusttram— Belgium's coastal tram

The Belgian Coast Tram is reckoned to be the longest tram line in the world, following almost the entire Belgian coastline from De Panne, on the French border, to Knokke, on the Dutch border. There are a total of 70 stops over 68 km and all the coastal towns and villages can be visited.

It starts right near the border between France and Belgium in the city De Panne and stops in the city Knokke-Heist at the border between Belgium and Netherlands. It crosses sixteen major cities and has seventy stops. A big part of this tramline curves along the North Sea, which definitely offers wonderful landscapes.

The first part of this line was built early in 1885, while the rest was finished after the First World War, with small adjustments in the last decade. The tram comes every twenty minutes in offseason and every ten in the summer. Thousands of Belgians use it every day to commute.

The trams are new, silent and they get you from one end to the other in approximately two hours and twenty minutes. They run from 6:00 am until almost midnight and stops at every station, although you should be careful to push the button and let the driver know you want to get out.

Test Your MEMORY

1. What is land transport?

2. Write briefly the history of land transport.

3. Describe briefly the categories of land transportation.

4. Name the types of land transport vehicles.

5. Describe roads and highways.

6. Write briefly about traffic control.

7. Write the advantages of land transport.

8. Write the disadvantages of land transport.

9. Write about land transport's impact on environment.

10. Write briefly about two famous cars.

11. Write briefly about two famous trains.

12. Write briefly about two famous bikes.

Index

A
automobiles 4, 7, 8, 9, 12, 15, 21

B
bicycle 5, 8, 11
Blue Train 27
Bugatti Veyron 21
bus 4, 7, 8, 9

C
camel caravan 4
car 3, 6, 7, 8, 9, 12, 13, 21, 22, 27
Conestoga wagon 4, 8

E
environment 3, 18, 29
Eurostar 25

F
four-wheeled carriages 4

H
highways 12

K
Kusttram 30

L
land transport 3, 4, 8, 10, 17, 18, 20
lectica 6

M
motorcycle 8, 11, 28

O
omnibuses 4, 8, 9

P
plaustrum 6
prairie schooner 4, 8

R
raeda 6
rickshaws 7
roads 3, 4, 5, 7, 10, 12, 13, 18, 20, 23
Rolls-Royce Phantom 22

S
Shinkansen (Bullet trains) 26
stagecoaches 4, 8
Suzuki Hayabusa 29

T
Tata trucks 23
taxi 8, 9
traffic lights 15
train 8, 10, 25, 26, 27
tram 8, 10, 13, 30
Trans Siberian Express 24
two-wheeled carts 4, 6, 8

V
velotaxis 7
Volvo trucks 23

W
wagons 4, 5, 6

PEGASUS ENCYCLOPEDIA LIBRARY

Transport
WATER TRANSPORT

Edited by: Pallabi B. Tomar
Managing editor: Tapasi De
Designed by: Vijesh Chahal, Anil Kumar and Rohit Kumar
Illustrated by: Suman S. Roy, Tanoy Choudhury
Colouring done by: Vinay Kumar, Sonu, Kiran Kumari & Pradeep Kumar

WATER TRANSPORT

CONTENTS

Introduction 3

History of water transport 4

Types of ships 6

Important water transport routes 12

Seaport 13

Advantages of water transport 15

Disadvantages 18

Importance to economy 19

World's famous ships 20

Test Your Memory 31

Index 32

Introduction

Introduction

Like road transport, water transport has been around for thousands of years. The first kinds of water transport were probably some types of canoes cut out from tree trunks.

Early sea transportation was accomplished with ships that were either rowed or used the wind for propulsion and sometimes a combination of the two.

Ship transport was frequently used as a mechanism for conducting warfare. Military use of the seas and waterways is covered in greater detail under the navy.

Water transport has dominated in transport services for centuries until the emergence of air transport. Nowadays, ships have been designed to be much faster and to be more competitive. Although relatively slow, modern water or sea transport are significantly less costly to use compared to air transport for carrying a large number of passengers for short inter-island trips and quantities of non-perishable goods in transcontinental routes.

> Ships and boats are very old inventions. Archaeologists think that people first made journeys in small boats 50,000 years ago.

3

WATER TRANSPORT

History of water transport

As man overcame the boundaries of land travel, his curiosity about the world around him increased. To his aid, man had developed a means of travelling on water even before he had domesticated the horse. The origin of the **dugout boat** is one of history's great mysteries. Historians are unable to pinpoint when or where the very first water vessel was set afloat. But the addition of the boat changed the face of transportation. Boats allowed man to, for the first time ever, cross bodies of water without getting wet!

Over time, the simple boat started including a large square piece of cloth which was mounted on a central pole. This cloth, called a sail, would turn the boat into a sail-propelled ship. This new addition gave man the ability to use waterways as a means of swift travel from one place to another, and even to travel against the current of rivers. However, the evolution of water travel didn't stop with the sail. Ships would eventually take on a sleekness as they increased in size. Before long, they would add oars and rudders and then deck covers. By Greek and Roman times, ships had grown clunky shipboard towers as well, which developed over time into the medieval stern and forecastles. By the late medieval era, these castles were built solid, as a part of the ship's basic structure. Then, by the Renaissance and the Age of Exploration which followed, ships had gained tiers of rigging and sails, becoming sleek and speedy.

Then, in the 1800s, ships began to shed their sails on the rivers once again. The advent of automation was changing transportation forever. The very first automation in ships was the cumbersome paddlewheel.

> Archaeologists don't really know when sailing boats were invented. However, the Ancient Egyptians sailed boats made out of the reeds growing along the River Nile over 5,000 years ago.

History of water transport

Due to their bulky form and inability to turn easily, paddlewheel boats were confined to river travel, where they would experience calmer currents and need less manoeuvrability.

After the paddlewheel came the steamship. These vessels used coal or wood burned to heat water, which in turn created the steam pressure used to work the pistons which moved the ship. The steamship was to enjoy a long and trusted run on both rivers and seas. Then, in 1912, the first diesel-powered ship, the **MS Selandia**, was launched. That diesel engine design was to become the industrial and military standard until after World War II.

Then, in 1958, the first nuclear powered ship was launched. However, nuclear power was soon discarded by industry as too expensive and risky, though it would continue to find use in the military community.

A triangular sail called a lateen sail was invented around 300 BC.

The landmark inventions in water transportation are:

- Cornelis Drebbel invented the first submarine (1620 AD)
- First practical steamboat demonstrated by Marquis Claude (1783 AD)
- Steamboat invented (1787 AD)
- First diesel-powered ship (1912 AD)
- Hovercraft invented (1956 AD)
- First nuclear powered ship launched (1958 AD)

WATER TRANSPORT

Types of ships

Cargo Ships

A cargo ship or freighter is any sort of ship or vessel that carries cargo, goods and materials from one port to another. Thousands of cargo carriers ply the world's seas and oceans each year; they handle the bulk of international trade. Cargo ships are usually specially designed for the task, often being equipped with cranes and other mechanisms to load and unload, and come in all sizes. Today, they are almost always built of welded steel, and generally have a life expectancy of 25 to 30 years before being scrapped.

Tankers

Tankers are ships that carries a cargo of liquid in bulk; oil and its products, liquefied gases, chemicals, wine and water. Tankers are a relatively new concept dating from the later years of the 19th century. Before this, technology had simply not supported the idea of carrying bulk liquids. Liquids were usually loaded in casks.

Tanker

Tankers can range in size of capacity from several hundred tons, which include vessels for servicing small harbours and coastal settlements, to several hundred thousand tons for long-range haulage.

Oil tankers are the largest ships on the seas and have developed from the L.C.C. (large crude carrier) to the V.L.C.C. (very large crude carrier) and then to the U.L.C.C (ultra large crude carrier).

Different products require different handling and transport. Thus special types of tankers have been built, such as 'chemical tankers', 'oil tankers' and 'LNG carriers' (a tanker designed to carry 'liquefied natural gas').

Cargo Ship

Types of ships

Hovercraft

Industrial Ships

Industrial ships are those whose function is to carry out an industrial process at sea. A fishing-fleet mother ship that processes fish into fillets, canned fish or fish meal is an example. In addition, some hazardous industrial wastes are incinerated far at sea on ships fitted with the necessary incinerators and supporting equipment. In many cases, industrial ships can be recognized by the structures necessary for their function. For example, incinerator ships are readily identified by their incinerators and discharge stacks.

Hovercraft

A hovercraft is an air cushion vehicle (ACV) that flies above any surface on a cushion of air. It is powered by an engine that provides both the lift cushion and the thrust for forward or reverse movement. It is a true multi-terrain, year-round vehicle that can make the transition from land to water without touching the surface.

The hovercraft was invented by Christopher Cockerell, an English electronic engineer in the 1950s. The first full-sized hovercraft, the SRN1 was not built and ready for testing until May 28, 1959.

Depending upon the effects of terrain and weather, the average speed of a hovercraft is 56 km/h. It is faster on ice or when going downwind, slower when on dense grass or rough surfaces, or when there is a head wind.

The idea for the hydrofoil (a waterborne vessel that uses underwater wings to generate lift in the same way that a plane uses wings to generate lift in air) was thought of in 1881. However, the first hydrofoil was not tested until 1905.

WATER TRANSPORT

Most modern ships are pushed along by a propeller. It was patented in 1836 and soon replaced paddle wheels.

Cruise Ships

A cruise ship is a passenger ship used for pleasure voyages. Transportation in such cases is not the prime purpose, as cruise ships operate mostly on routes that return passengers to their originating port.

Cruise ships are organized much like floating hotels, with a complete hospitality staff in addition to the usual ship's crew. It is not uncommon for the most luxurious ships to have more crew and staff than passengers.

The number of cruise tourists worldwide in 2005 was estimated at some 14 million. The main region for cruising was North America (70 per cent of cruises), where the Caribbean islands were the most popular destinations.

Ferries

Ferries are vessels of any size that carry passengers and (in many cases) their vehicles travel on fixed routes over short cross-water passages. Vessels vary greatly in size and in quality of accommodations. Some on longer runs offer overnight cabins and even come close to equalling the accommodation standards of cruise ships. All vessels typically load vehicles aboard one or more decks via low-level side doors or by stern or bow ramps much like those found on roll-on/roll-off cargo ships.

The typical vessel has propellers, rudders, control stations and loading ramps at both ends. It is usually wide enough to handle four vehicle lanes abreast and may accommodate up to 100 four-wheeled vehicles.

Types of ships

Specialist Ships

It is intended to encompass classifications such as icebreakers and research vessels, many of which are owned by the government. Neither type needs to be large in size, since no cargo is to be carried. However, icebreakers are usually wide in order to make a wide swath through ice, and they have high propulsive power in order to overcome the resistance of the ice layer. Icebreakers also are characterized by strongly sloping bow profiles, especially near the waterline, so that they can wedge their way up onto thick ice and crack it from the static weight placed upon it. To protect the hull against damage, the waterline of the ship must be reinforced by layers of plating and supported by heavy stiffeners.

Damage to propellers is also an icebreaking hazard. Propellers are usually given protection by a hull geometry that tends to divert ice from them, and they are often built with individually replaceable blades to minimize the cost of repairing damage. Electric transmission of power between engines and propellers is also common practice, since it allows precise control and an easy diversion of power to another propeller from one that may be jammed by chunks of broken ice.

Research vessels, also called RV or R/V, are ships specifically designed and equipped to conduct research at sea. Research vessels are often distinguished externally by cranes and winches for handling nets and small underwater vehicles. Often they are fitted with bow and stern side thrusters in order to enable them to remain in a fixed position in spite of unfavourable winds and currents. Internally, research vessels are usually characterized by laboratory and living spaces for the research personnel.

WATER TRANSPORT

Container Ships

Container ships can carry more than 13,000 containers, which are packed with all sorts of different goods and products, food, drink, chemicals and consumer items. The container concept has revolutionised sea trade. The container ship's superstructure, bridge and main engines are often placed towards the stern, leaving a large unobstructed deck space for cargo hatchways or containers. Nearly all goods can be transported in containers, which are built in standard sizes usually of 6 m and 12 m in lengths. Containers are packed ashore at factories or inland depots, carried by road or rail to a port, shipped and only opened when they reach their destination.

Barge-carrying Ships

An extension of the container ship concept is the barge-carrying ship. In this concept, the container is itself a floating vessel, usually about 18 m long by about 9 m wide, which is loaded aboard the ship in one of two ways; either it is lifted over the stern by a high-

In 1889, Morgan Roberts wrote 'The Wreck of the Titan'. It tells the story of a massive luxury liner, called the Titan, which hit an iceberg and sank. The Titanic did exactly that 14 years later and more than 1,500 of the passengers were drowned!

capacity shipboard gantry crane, or the ship is partially submerged so that the barges can be floated aboard via a gate in the stern.

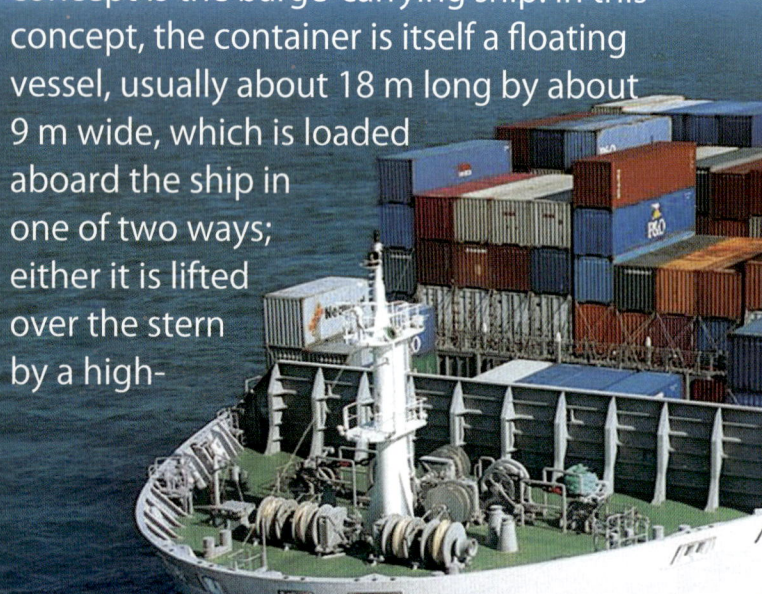
Container ship

Types of ships

Roll-on/roll-off Ships

Roll-on/roll-off ships (RORO) are specially designed ships, used to carry wheeled and tracked vehicles like cars, tractors, trucks, cranes as their major cargo load. The modern day RORO ships may even carry tanks, choppers, jets, etc. They have their own ramps or use shores ramps to load-unload the vehicles and then carry them from place to place. The cargo usually varies in height and width and hence the below deck and volume utilization is comparatively lesser than other ships and hence can be costlier as well. So they are the preferred transport for military vehicles and other such specialized jobs.

Astonishing fact

Over the years, ships and aeroplanes have vanished in the Bermuda Triangle, without trace of any wreckage. In 1880, a ship called the HMS Atalanta disappeared together with 290 crew members.

Dry Bulk Ships

Dry bulk ships transport large volume cargoes in ship loads. Major dry bulk commodities consist of industrial raw materials including iron ore, coal, grain, bauxite and alumina. Minor bulks such as soya beans/meal, steel products, phosphate rocks and sulphur also accounts for a significant part of the dry bulk trade.

Dry bulk carriers are generally designed for simplicity and cheapness. However some of the small vessels are of higher technical designs in order to trade special cargoes such as cements and rocks. These vessels are somewhat similar to multipurpose vessels in both size and design.

WATER TRANSPORT

Important water transport routes

Shipping routes reflect world trade flows. Sailings are most numerous and most frequent on routes where trade volumes are largest and demand is therefore the greatest.

Some of the important sea routes are:

> In 1935 the French warship 'Le Terrible' set a world record for speed reaching a commendable 45.25 knots (83.42 km/h) during trials.

North Atlantic Route

It is a sea route connecting Atlantic Pacific oceans through Canada. It is the busiest sea route in the world.

The Suez Canal Route

This canal connects the Mediterranean Sea with the Gulf of Suez and the Red Sea. It was opened in 1869. Earlier one had to go via the Cape of Good Hope to go to England which took almost 6 months but this canal has reduced the time taken. Now it takes only two months to reach England. It is around 160 km long.

The Panama Canal Route

The Panama Canal became operational in the year 1914. This canal connects the Atlantic Ocean with the Pacific Ocean. This canal has considerably reduced the travelling time between the two oceans. Earlier the ships had to go via Cape Horn.

There are well-established routes to the Middle East, India, Australia and New Zealand, Central and South America, as well as to East and West Africa.

In-bulk trade routes reflect the places of origin and consumption of the commodities carried. For example, many of the main oil routes begin in the Middle East and end in developed countries where demand for oil is greatest.

Seaport

A seaport is a facility which can accommodate ships which go out to sea. Seaports can be found in natural and artificial harbours along many coastlines in the world, and they have a variety of fixtures including cranes to help ships handle cargo, and docks for ships to attach to. Seaports are of economic and strategic importance to the nations which hold them, because they can be used for everything from shipping out a nation's consumer products to loading up troop ships to sail to war.

A typical seaport includes equipment and facilities for handling and storing cargo, such as warehouses and cranes, along with amenities which are designed to appeal to people coming into port, such as restaurants and hotels. Ship building and repair companies are typically located near ports for the convenience of their clients, and sea ports may also have facilities for quarantine and other special needs; a well-designed port may allow people to get everything they need without straying more than a few blocks away from their ship. Some seaports are primarily focused on cargo and commercial trade, while others cater to passenger boats like cruise ships, and many provide facilities for a mixture of uses.

> Commissioned in 1797, the 'USS Constitution' won several sea battles during the American War of Independence. Amazingly she still remains on the roster of the United States Navy today as a training ship manned by a crew of 50 to 80 navy sailors.

WATER TRANSPORT

The strategic importance of a seaport can change over time. Some ports have been lost due to erosion or other issues which have caused the port to vanish or become innavigable. Others have become less important because they are no longer on major trade routes or because a nation's production of cargo has declined, making the port less profitable for shippers. The most valuable ports tend to be warm water ports, in which the water in and around the port does not freeze in the winter, allowing the port to be used year-round.

One of the most famous seaports of the world is the **National Historic Seaport of Baltimore** which is dates back to almost 300 years. Some other famous cruise ports are Boston Port-U.S.A., Norfolk Port- U.S.A., New York Port- America, Montreal Port- Canada, Philadelphia Port- U.S.A., etc.

In all there are a total of 4206 ports in the 195 countries in the world. The number of ports have increased keeping in line with the growth in sea traffic and the size of the vessels. Many of these ports serve as economy drivers for these countries and many are known for their most efficient connections across the world by means of water. The shipping industry thus forms the baseline for most part of world's export and import.

> **In the 1400s full rigging was developed. Full-rigged ships had two or three masts with square and triangular sails.**

Advantages of water transport

Industrialized nations of the world are concerned about the environmental impacts of their activities. Studies compare the environmental impact of using rail, truck or barging for commercial transportation. Though results vary depending on the size of the barges used in the comparison, the conclusions have been the same. Barges using the inland waterways carry greater volumes for the same amount of fuel and with less environmental impact than either trucks or railcars.

It is safe

Transporting cargo safely is an important measure of environmental responsibility, and water transport has the fewest number of accidents, fatalities and injuries as compared to truck or rail.

In the 1400s and 1500s European explorers, such as Christopher Columbus, sailed small full-rigged ships across the oceans.

Water transportation has definite advantages over competitive modes. It generally involves less urban exposure than either truck or rail, operates on a system that has few crossing junctures; and is relatively remote from population centres, all factors that reduce both the number and impact of waterway incidents.

Truck and rail tank car spills occur more often than barge spills. Barges, because of their much larger capacity, require far fewer units than either rail or truck to move an equivalent amount of cargo, and so the chance of a spill is less likely. Also, design features of barges such as double-hulls and navigational aids help reduce accident frequency.

WATER TRANSPORT

Produces little air and noise pollution

Some of the most pervasive and intrusive sources of noise and air pollution are transportation systems.

Noise levels, with road traffic the chief offender, have been rising. Air pollution comes from a wide variety of man-made and natural sources, with fossil fuel combustion the largest contributor. Air pollution caused by transportation includes pollutants directly emitted by engines as well as secondary pollutants formed by chemical reactions. Road traffic is, by far, the greatest source of air emissions.

Water transport, conversely, causes far less air pollution than trucking, and less or comparable amounts than rail. Cumulatively, it has a relatively minor effect on air quality, consumes much less energy (and as a result, produces less air pollution). For the most part, waterway operations are conducted away from population centres, which reduce the impact of its exhaust emissions. Towboats operate well away from shore, with the sound of their engines muffled below the water line, and any noise levels are hardly audible beyond the immediate area of the tow.

Causes little congestion

Other impacts of traffic congestion are accidents, increased energy consumption, environmental damage, increased commuting times and greater social tension. Water transport, in contrast, does not have congestion problems, and seldom causes them for others. The fact is that far from being congested, water transport system is under utilized.

> A yacht is a vessel used for private cruising, racing or other non-commercial purposes. The lengths of yachts generally range from 8 m up to dozens of metres (hundreds of feet).

Advantages of water transport

Has minimal land use

Trains rumble through cities and trucks travel on streets and highways. Barges, on the other hand, quietly make their way along isolated waterways.

Most of the navigation way for water transport is provided by nature itself. So water transport is less likely than other transport forms to compete for land area for its navigation. Extensive land area can be taken up by new highways and railroad corridors, but apart from a few connections and waterside terminals, waterways pre-empt very little land.

A canoe is a small slender boat; about 5 m long, usually pointed at both ends, and is generally paddled by its occupants. The modern canoe is meant to hold 2-3 people, but ancient peoples built canoes large enough to carry many people and cargo.

Produces multiple benefits

Transporting bulk commodities by water has many other positive benefits and many beneficiaries.

When a new navigation project is completed, it benefits many areas including water transportation. The other major beneficiaries of developed waterway systems include recreation, flood control, public water supply, irrigation and industrial use, all uses that can be as important as the navigation project itself. Navigation not only creates opportunities for new industries, but may also change trade patterns that can have a major economic impact on local and regional development.

WATER TRANSPORT

Disadvantages

Slow Speed: Sea transport is not suitable for goods urgently needed because of its slow speed. So, not all types of goods can be transported by sea.

Documentation: Documents involved in transporting goods by sea are more in number and are very complex.

Other costs: Expenses for insurance premium, packing costs, and storage and port charges are very high and as a result increase the cost price of goods.

A row boat is a small boat that is propelled by oars. The boat can be of wooden or aluminium construction. A person sits facing the rear of the boat and pulls the oars towards his body, effectively driving the boat forward through the water.

It provides services to limited areas.

Canals maybe expensive to build and maintain.

Special maintenance for water tightness of boat is required.

It is difficult to monitor exact location of goods in transit.

Importance to economy

Increase in economic activity

If a country has a sufficient and sound infrastructure in the form of ports and waterways, the economic activity increases because many ships with tons of goods move in and out of the harbours of the country.

Increase in foreign exchange

Water transport increases foreign trade, as it increases the imports and exports of merchandise from one to the other parts of the world. International trade flourishes and trading partners are benefited a lot.

Decrease in transportation cost

Transportation cost reduces too much. Thus goods become cheap which improves the international trade between the various nations of the world.

Increase in government revenue

When foreign trade increases, it not only benefits general public, but it also becomes a great source of revenue for the government by way of customs duties.

Increase in employment opportunities

Many people get jobs in the shipping industry, as in loading and unloading goods from ships. Thus directly and indirectly lots of jobs are created. This increases the general welfare of the people of the country.

A steamer or steamship, is known as such because its primary method of propulsion is steam power, which typically drives propellers. Smaller steamboats use steam power to drive paddle-wheels.

WATER TRANSPORT

World's famous ships

Supertanker-Knock Nevis

Knock Nevis was a supertanker and the longest ship ever built. Before her final journey as the MV Mont she was known as the Knock Nevis and was a Norwegian owned supertanker. Prior to that, she was known as Seawise Giant, Happy Giant and Jahre Viking. She was 458 m in length and 69 m in width, making her the largest ship in the world. She was built between 1979 and 1981 but was damaged during the Iran-Iraq War while transiting the Strait of Hormuz. She sank and was declared a total loss. Shortly after Iran-Iraq war, Norman International bought the wreckage of the ship, repaired and refloated her in 1991. After that she was used as an immobile offshore platform for the oil industry. In 2009 the vessel was sold to Amber Development Corporation, and renamed MV Mont for her final journey to Alang, Gujarat, India in December 2009 where she was beached and scrapped.

This sea giant was so large that four football (soccer) fields could be laid end to end on her deck. She surpassed the height of the Empire State Building in New York City (443 m high) and Petronas Towers in Kuala Lumpur (424 m high). She sat 24.6 m in the water when fully loaded, which made it impossible for her to navigate even through the English Channel, let alone man-made canals at Suez and Panama!

Container Ship-Emma Maersk

Emma Maersk is a container ship owned by the A. P. Moller-Maersk Group. It is the world's largest container ship, longest ship currently in service and is propelled by the largest diesel engine ever manufactured. She is bigger than any aircraft carrier and manages to carry 15000 containers with only a crew of 13! She was designed for high sea travels only and unable to negotiate the Suez or Panama canals. She has a top speed of 55.8 km/h and takes about 4 days to reach Asia from US.

Emma Maersk is able to carry around 11,000 twenty-foot equivalent units (TEU) according to the Maersk company's method of calculating capacity, which is about 1,400 more containers than any other ship is capable of carrying. The vessel is 397 m long, 56 m wide, has a depth of 30 m and deadweight of 156,907 tons.

The Emma Maersk is powered by a Wärtsilä-Sulzer 14RTFLEX96-C engine, currently the world's largest single diesel unit, weighing 2,300 tons and capable of 109,000 horsepower (82 MW). The ship has several features to protect the environment. This includes recycling the exhaust, mixed with fresh air, back into the engine for reuse. This not only increases efficiency by as much as 12 per cent but also reduces engine emissions.

WATER TRANSPORT

Ocean Liner-Queen Mary 2

The Queen Mary 2 is unique. Queen Mary 2 is not only a feat in engineering, but also in size. This mighty vessel is the largest, longest and most expensive ocean liner ever built - an impressive title indeed! She is the only transatlantic ocean liner left in service. She is huge, fast, strong and has numerous unique aspects to her design that define her as an ocean liner rather than just a cruise ship.

After arriving in her home port of Southampton on Boxing Day 2003, Queen Mary 2 was named by the Queen Elizabeth II on the 8th of January before setting out on her maiden voyage to Florida on the 12th. She and her sister ship the Queen Elizabeth 2, were the only 2 true ocean liners left in the world.

On 12 January 2004, the Queen Mary 2 set sail on her maiden voyage from Southampton, England to Fort Lauderdale, Florida in the United States, carrying 2,620 passengers. On 10 January 2007, the QM2 started her first world cruise, circling the globe in 81 days.

Famous passengers or guests of the QM2 include Queen Elizabeth II, Prince Philip, Duke of Edinburgh, former French President Jacques Chirac, former British Prime Minister Tony Blair, former US president George H. W. Bush, comedian and actor John Cleese, actor Richard Dreyfuss, author and editor Harold Evans, director George Lucas, singer Carly Simon, singer Rod Stewart, CBS Evening News anchor Katie Couric and financier Donald Trump.

World's famous ships

The gondola is a world famous symbol of Venice. It is a traditional, flat-bottomed rowing boat. The main role is to carry tourists on rides at fixed prices. The gondola is moved forward by a person, the gondolier, who stands facing the bow and rows with a forward stroke followed by a backward stroke.

Bulk Carrier-Berge Stahl

The Berge Stahl is the largest bulk carrier ship in the world. An iron ore carrier, the Berge Stahl has a capacity of 364,767 metric tons of deadweight. She was built in 1986 by Hyundai Heavy Industries. The Berge Stahl is 343 m long, has a beam, or width of 65 m, and a draft, or depth in the water of 23 m.

Her Hyundai B&W 7L90MCE diesel engine is 9 m high, drives a single 9 m screw, and puts out 27,610 horsepower (20.59 MW), has a top speed of 13.5 knots, and has a 9 m high rudder.

Because of her massive size, the Berge Stahl can only tie up, fully loaded, at two ports in the world, hauling ore from the Terminal Marítimo de Ponta da Madeira in Brazil to the Europoort near Rotterdam in the Netherlands. Even at these ports, passage must be timed to coincide with high tides to prevent the ship running aground. The Berge Stahl makes this trip about ten times each year, or a round-trip about every five weeks.

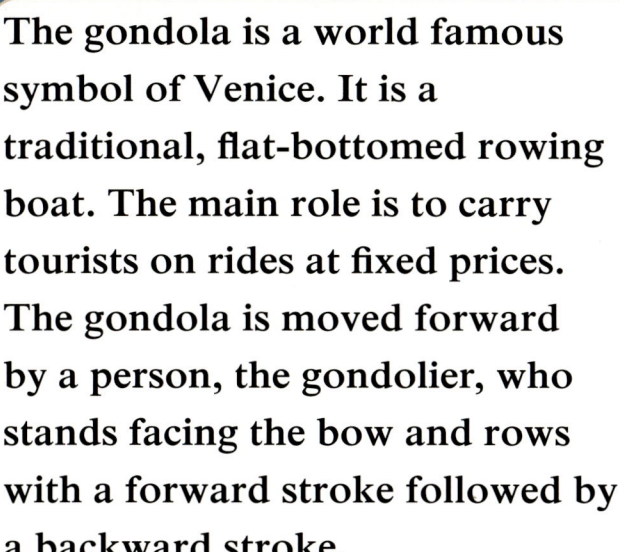

WATER TRANSPORT

Aircraft Carrier-USS Enterprise (CVN-65)

The USS Enterprise (CVN-65) is the longest naval vessel at 342 m. Due to size, she is often referred to as the 'Big E.' The Enterprise is the only aircraft carrier propelled by more than two nuclear reactors; with eight, each replaces one boiler. In addition, she is the only carrier with four rudders instead of two, and the first nuclear-powered aircraft carrier to transit the Suez Canal.

The Enterprise was commissioned in 1961 and her first air operations came in 1962 when a Vought F8 Crusader attempted a landing and catapult launch from her deck. That same year, she served the role of tracking and measuring station for Lieutenant Colonel John H. Glenn's space capsule Friendship 7. In 1964, the Enterprise, as part of the world's first nuclear-powered powerhouse (designated as Task Force One), took part in Operation Sea Orbit. It was a 65 day, 30,216 mile trip around the world, without stops for replenishment or refuelling.

The only ship of her class, Enterprise is the second-oldest vessel in commission in the United States Navy. She was originally scheduled for decommissioning in 2014 or 2015, but the National Defence Authorization Act for Fiscal Year 2010 slated the ship's retirement for 2013, when she will have served for 51 consecutive years, the most of any U.S. aircraft carrier.

Jet ski is a small, jet-propelled vehicle that skims across the surface of water and typically is ridden like a motorcycle. It relies on a gas-powered engine to propel themselves and a few riders through the water.

World's famous ships

Allure of the Seas

The world's largest cruise ship 'Allure of the Seas,' is a new ship of Royal Caribbean International. The 'Allure of the Seas' is an architectural fantasy on the sea. It spans 360 m from bow to stern, and its height from sea level Is 72 m. It welghs 600 tons – 12 times more than the Eiffel Tower.

There are altogether 16 decks and 2,704 passenger cabins in the vessel, which maximum capacity is 6,360 passengers and a crew of 2,100. Aside from a two-deck high dance hall, a 1380-seat theatre and an ice skating rink, a number of pools, spas, gyms, it also houses bars, restaurants and cafes as well as a shopping street with a park with trees.

It names the Rising Tide Bar as one of its showpieces – an elliptical restaurant platform accommodating 50 customers that ascends and descends a vertical distance of 10 m between the central park and promenade.

> A water taxi is a small boat used for public transportation. Service maybe scheduled with multiple stops, operating in a similar manner to a bus or a taxi.

WATER TRANSPORT

U.S.S. Constitution

The Constitution, called 'Old Ironsides' because cannonballs could not penetrate her tough oak sides, was one of the first of the original six frigates that made up the U.S. Navy. It is the oldest warship of the US Navy and the oldest commissioned warship afloat in the world. Still afloat after 213 years, she had an usually long service life, having remained in commission on and off between 1797 all the way to the Civil War, after which she was made a training ship and continued sailing periodically right up to her final decommissioning in 1881. During that time she fought in two conflicts: the First Barbary War—when she battled real pirates—and the War of 1812, during which she distinguished herself by defeating the British frigates HMS Guerriere and HMS Java. It was those engagements that gave her something of a reputation as a ship that could take on the British in a head-to-head fight, which was no small feat when one considers that the British Royal Navy was the largest and most powerful in the world at the time. Her fame saved her from the wrecking yard and in 1907 she began serving as a museum ship. Old Ironsides has been restored, refurbished and otherwise rebuilt so many times, it is said her keel is the only part of the original ship that remains, the rest having being replaced numerous times over the decades. She is also a still officially commissioned warship, with a sixty-man crew who are all active duty members of the United States Navy.

World's famous ships

MV Blue Marlin—World's largest transport ship

The MV Blue Marlin is a Dutch ship that was built in the year 2000 as a float-on/float-off or a heavy lift vessel that can be partially submerged. The Blue Marlin's cargo carrying capacity is around 30,000 tons and the ease with which the 154 m and 6,800 ton USS Cole was shipped from one part of the world to another, proves that the ship was designed to endure and carry cargo through.

The main reason the MV Blue Marlin was constructed was to provide a sort of base or anchorage to oil rigs. It has to be noted that the heavy lift vessel has several tiers which lower themselves into the water as and when required. This feature is the main USP of the Dutch naval vessel. Because of these tiers, the weight load of the cargo above is adequately balanced without any damage to it.

It has to be noted that all such heavy lift vessels including the Blue Marlin have cranes to lift and place the cargo on top of them. The total lift-off capacity of a crane at the very first lift is around 100 tons. This, once again proves the authenticity and reliability of a heavy lift vessel and more importantly, of the Blue Marlin in particular.

The main objective of heavy lift vessels such as the Blue Marlin is to provide cargo carrying facility to warships to ports and dry-docks for the purpose of repairing. It was only with the help of such a technology, that a very important naval warship was able to get restored back for a new naval life.

WATER TRANSPORT

Largest yacht— Eclipse

With a reported price tag of nearly $1.2 billion and a 170 m length, the Eclipse is not only the largest yacht, but also the most expensive. Russian billionaire Roman Abramovich's yacht Eclipse has received a huge amount of industry attention, not just for its size but for the celebrity of its owner.

> A submarine is a large vessel that operates below the water surface. The nickname of a submarine is sub, and the word submarine means under the water. It is a large, cylinder shaped 'boat' that is used for military, tourism or oil purposes.

The billionaire's mega yacht was constructed by the German ship construction company Blohm & Voss. It has two helicopter landing pads, its own mini submarine, 2 hot tubs and 2 regular pools and a cinema. The newest and most expensive yacht in the world also has anti rocket systems for preventing terrorist attacks and is fully bullet-proof. It also comes equipped with three launch boats, and a mini-submarine that is capable of submerging to 50 m. About 70 crew members are needed to operate the yacht.

As a new addition never before seen on mega yachts the Eclipse boosts a system that uses lasers to make it impossible for paparazzi to take photos. When activated the lasers automatically find all camera lenses pointing at the yacht and shine a laser on them thus making photographing impossible.

World's famous ships

Yamato

Yamato, a Japanese battleship, is the world's largest battleship ever built, also mounting the largest calibre main armament ever built, at 18.1 inches in diameter. Yamato is named after the ancient Japanese Yamato Province, was a battleship of the Imperial Japanese Navy. She and her sister ship the Musashi were the largest, heaviest and most powerful battleships ever constructed, displacing 72,800 tons at full load, and armed with nine 46 cm (18.1 inch) main guns. The ship held special significance for the Empire of Japan as a symbol of the nation's naval power, and it's sinking by US aircraft in the final days of the war during the suicide **Operation Ten-Go** is sometimes considered symbolic of Japan's defeat itself.

Bismarck

Bismarck, a German battleship was one of the most famous warships of the 2nd World War. It was named after the 19th

century German chancellor Otto von Bismarck. It displaced more than 50,000 tons fully loaded and was the largest warship then commissioned. Her chief claim to fame came from the Battle of the Denmark Strait in May 1941 during which the battle cruiser HMS Hood, flagship of the Home Fleet and pride of the Royal Navy, was sunk within several minutes. In response, British Prime Minister Winston Churchill issued the order to 'Sink the Bismarck', spurring a relentless pursuit by the Royal Navy. Two days later, with safer waters almost in reach, Fleet Air Arm aircraft torpedoed Bismarck and jammed her rudder, allowing heavy British units to catch up with her. In the ensuing battle on the morning of May 27, 1941, Bismarck was heavily attacked for nearly three hours before sinking.

WATER TRANSPORT

Titanic

No other ship has captured the world's attention, quite like the Titanic. Constructed to be unsinkable, this first class ocean liner set sail on April 10, 1912. The world had awaited the maiden voyage of this luxury liner for months.

On the night of 14 April 1912, Titanic hit an iceberg, and sank two hours and forty minutes later, early on April 15, 1912. At the time of her launching in 1912, she was the largest passenger steamship in the world. The sinking resulted in the deaths of 1,517 people, one of the deadliest maritime disasters in history and by far the most famous. The discovery of the wreck in 1985 has made Titanic persistently famous in the years since.

Victoria

Victoria became famous in history because it was the first ship to successfully circumnavigate the world. The voyage was lead by Magellan and was accompanied by four other ships. Of this fleet of five, Victoria was the only ship to complete the voyage. Magellan himself was killed in the Philippines. The four other ships were Trinidad (110 tons, crew 55), San Antonio (120 tons, crew 60), Concepcion (90 tons, crew 45) and Santiago (75 tons, crew 32). Trinidad, Magellan's flagship, Concepcion, and Santiago were wrecked; San Antonio deserted the expedition before the Strait of Magellan and returned to Europe on her own. Victoria was rated a ship, as were all the others except Trinidad, which was a caravel.

A catamaran is a type of boat or ship consisting of two hulls joined by a frame. Catamarans can be sailed or engine-powered. The catamaran was the invention of the paravas, a fishing community in the southern coast of Tamil Nadu, India.

Test Your MEMORY

1. What do you mean by water transport?

2. Write briefly about the history of water transport.

3. Define the types of water transport.

4. Name the types of ships.

5. Name the important water transport routes.

6. What are seaports?

7. Write about the advantages of water transport.

8. Write about the disadvantages of water transport.

9. Write about water transport's importance to economy.

10. Write briefly about the Knock Nevis.

11. Name the largest bulk carrier ship in the world.

12. Name the largest yacht in the world.

WATER TRANSPORT

Index

A
Allure of the seas 25

B
Berge Stahl 23
Bismarck 29

C
cargo ship 6
container ships 10

D
deck covers 4
dry bulk ships 11
dugout boat 4

E
Eclipse 28
Emma Maersk 21

F
ferries 8

H
harbour 13
Hovercraft 5, 7

I
icebreakers 9
industrial ships 7

J
Jahre Viking 20

K
Knock Nevis 20

M
MV Blue Marlin 27

O
oars 4, 18
ocean liner 22, 30

P
paddlewheel boats 5

Q
Queen Mary 2 22

R
research vessels 9
rigging 4, 14
roll-on/roll-off ships (RORO) 11
rudders 4, 8, 24

S
sail 4, 5, 13, 22, 30
seaport 13, 14
steamship 5, 19, 30
stern 4, 8, 9, 10, 25

T
tankers 6
Titanic 10, 30

U
U.S.S. Constitution 26

V
Victoria 30

W
water transport 3, 4, 5, 12, 13, 15, 16, 17, 19

Y
Yamato 29

PEGASUS ENCYCLOPEDIA LIBRARY

Transport
TRUCKS

Edited by: Pallabi B. Tomar
Managing editor: Tapasi De
Designed by: Vijesh Chahal, Anil Kumar and Rohit Kumar
Illustrated by: Suman S. Roy, Tanoy Choudhury
Colouring done by: Vinay Kumar, Sonu, Kiran Kumari & Pradeep Kumar

TRUCKS

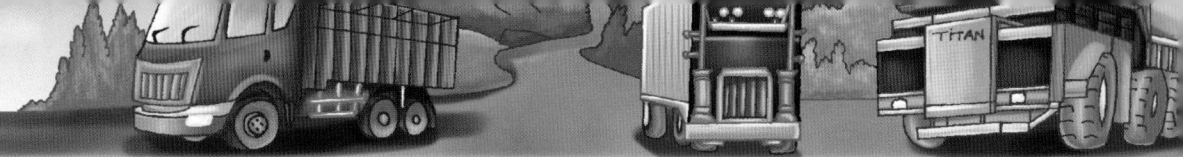

CONTENTS

Introduction 3

History 4

Types of trucks 7

Parts of a truck 10

Maintenance of trucks 14

Advantages 18

Disadvantages 19

Trucking industry 20

Famous truck manufacturers 23

Some famous trucks 26

Test Your Memory 31

Index 32

Introduction

Truck, derived from the Greek word 'trochos' meaning 'wheel' is a vehicle that carries goods and materials. While there are luxury cars to carry people around, there are trucks that carry large and heavy goods and materials from one place to another.

Unlike automobiles, which usually have a unibody construction, most trucks are built around a strong frame called a **chassis**. They come in all sizes, from the automobile-sized pickup truck to towering off-road mining trucks or heavy highway semi-trailers.

There are trucks that use gasoline engines, while other trucks use four stroke turbo intercooler diesel engines. Some trucks also use locomotive-type engines. There are military-type light trucks that are used for troop transport.

The term is most commonly used in American English and Australian English to refer to what earlier was called a motor truck, and in British English is often called a lorry or for bigger vehicles, a Heavy Goods Vehicle (HGV). This type of truck is a motor vehicle designed to carry goods, with a cab and a tray or compartment for carrying goods.

Industrial designer Viktor Schreckengost revolutionized the trucking industry in 1932 when he redesigned the standard truck's body by placing the cab right over the engine.

TRUCKS

History

As there were attempts to innovate machines to transport goods other than steam engines in the second half of the eighteenth century, what can be described as the first truck in history was born in 1896.

Built by Daimler-Motoren-Gesellschaft, the initial design was derived from the carts of the time, simply by removing the front of the animals intended for hooking and pulling with the assembly of the wheel axles of a two-cylinder engine for about 2200 cm3 which developed 6 horsepower and could propel the vehicle at a speed of 16 km/ h. The wheels were strictly made of wood with the outer rim of metal and also the braking system was the same used for the coaches.

Following the evolution of cars, manufacturers improved with the adoption of a closed body that protects the driver. The engine was positioned in front of the cockpit. Another important improvement concerns the transition to solid rubber tyres and the presence of the first diversification of the receptacles, now closed.

In the first two decades of the twentieth century the importance of trucks continued to increase. Other manufacturers were impoverished in the market, such as Fiat, which provided the first truck to the Royal Army, Fiat 15. The end of the twenties saw the first trucks equipped with shaft drive and the first equipped with tyres tube.

The Ford truck was introduced in 1925 after more than a 20 years research by Henry Ford.

History

Ford trucks have been the most consistent best selling vehicle for the Ford Motor Company.

The innovations introduced in the thirties were also very important for the continuation of the history of the truck. First, the engine, until then positioned behind the front axle, was taken much further in front and on the same axis, resulting in an immediate best weight distribution on the truck and a substantial increase in payload. The wooden wheels were in the meantime, completely abandoned in favour of metal wheels and brakes, until then limited usually to the front wheels, it also widened the rear of the vehicle. In the cities trucks made more and more deliveries. Even the engines were moving increasingly towards petrol and diesel.

The following decade saw the truck again at the centre of attention mainly for its work in the field of war. During the Second World War, it was the main vehicle for the transfer of troops and baggage on the various fronts and all the branch companies were engaged in manufacturing it to meet the huge demand which cropped up during that time.

After the World War II, companies returned again to design vehicles for civilian use. More and more trucks equipped with diesel engines hit the market, a remarkable step forward in energy.

TRUCKS

In the fifties the first engine had a turbocharger, and they had powers of average around 200 horsepower. Perhaps the only thing that had made great strides was taking care of its interior cabins, especially with regard to the acoustic and thermal insulation of the passenger. With the first movement of the driver directly above the engine room, driving conditions were certainly not favourable, especially in the warmer months of the year.

The importance of the driver was taken seriously only in later years with the study of new solutions to make the driving time as comfortable as possible. Among the solutions found were those of a higher thermal and sound insulation, a more ergonomic design of seats and using the power steering, anti-vibration supports the inclusion of suspension system between the cab and chassis, together with the emergence of the cabins and the presence of a bed room behind the seats allowing the driver to stay in overnight stops.

The seventies and eighties saw the research in the field of the driver's visibility to the outside, the introduction of rigid bars on the sides and rear to prevent other vehicles to be able to slide under the truck in an accident, the introduction of disc brakes more powerful and the presentation of the first air suspension that significantly improved the ride attitude.

In these same years also developed a technology that allowed carriers to remain in contact with each other and sometimes even their homes. It was very useful to report problems on the roads. Now almost all trucks for long journeys were fitted with a radio transceiver, the famous CB.

The last decade of the century saw an increasing emphasis on the ecological impact and the manufacturers devoted much of their ability to start engine production with fewer emissions and pollutants.

Astonishing fact

In the early days of the fire service, fire trucks were horse drawn. In those days nearly every firehouse had a resident Dalmatian. The job of the Dalmatian was to lead the horses to the fire and protect them from horse thieves.

Types of trucks

Haulage Trucks

Haulage trucks are heavy duty carriers used to carry parcels, courier and for logistics. Some are used to transport cars, two-wheelers and three-wheelers, bricks, sand and coal or as water/petrol tankers.

Rigid Trucks

Rigid trucks are sturdy and used as transit mixers, containers, acid tankers, recovery trucks, self-loading cranes and even as liquefied petroleum gas containers.

Tippers

Tippers are robust vehicles used for tipping operations in industries such as construction and building, mining and quarrying industry and the public service sector. They can be used for on or off-highway needs.

Dump Trucks

A dump truck or production truck is a truck used for transporting loose material (such as sand, gravel, or dirt) for construction. A typical dump truck is equipped with a hydraulically operated open-box bed hinged at the rear, the front of which can be lifted up to allow the contents to be deposited on the ground behind the truck at the site of delivery. They are used by municipal corporations and the building industry.

TRUCKS

Pickup Trucks

The capacity if this vehicle is limited to 788 kg. The number of items that can be loaded is eight at a maximum. It is usually used for payload items. It is mainly used for business purposes which includes the transportation of electronic products or products that are heavy and big.

Flatbed Trucks

A flatbed truck is a type of truck which can be either articulated or rigid. It has an entirely flat, level body with absolutely no sides or roof. This allows for quick and easy loading of goods, and consequently they are used to transport heavy loads that are not delicate or vulnerable to precipitation, such as construction equipment, and also for abnormal loads that require more space than is available on a closed body. Trucks of this type are considered ideal for transporting goods that need to be unloaded quickly from the sides as well as the rear.

Garbage Trucks

A Waste Collection Vehicle (WCV) is a truck specially designed to pick up smaller quantities of waste and haul it to landfills and other recycling or treatment facilities. They are a common sight in most urban areas.

Types of trucks

Panel Trucks

A panel truck is a windowless cargo van built on a truck chassis. It is a station wagon with no backseat and no side windows behind the front doors. They are frequently used for delivery of flowers, retail bakery products, diapers, laundry and other consumer conveniences.

Semi-Trailer Trucks

A semi-trailer truck is an articulated truck or lorry consisting of a towing engine (tractor in the U.S., prime mover in Australia, and truck in UK, Canada and New Zealand), and a semi-trailer (plus possible additional trailers) that carries the freight.

Volvo trucks are currently sold in more than 140 countries all over the world, but it all began with the first one rolling off the assembly line in 1928 in Sweden.

Tanker Trucks

A tanker truck is a motor vehicle designed to carry liquefied loads, dry bulk cargo or gasses on roads. The largest such vehicles are similar to railroad tank cars which are also designed to carry liquefied loads. Many variants exist due to the wide variety of liquids that can be transported. Tank trucks tend to be large; they may be insulated or non-insulated, pressurized or non-pressurized and designed for single or multiple loads (often by means of internal divisions in their tank).

9

Parts of a truck

Chassis

A truck chassis consists of two parallel U-shaped beams held together by cross members. It is usually made of steel, but can be made (whole or in part) of aluminium for a lighter weight. The chassis is the main structure of the truck, and the other parts are attached to it.

> **During World War II, Volvo was a main supplier to the Swedish Armed Forces, and thousands of their 'Roundnose' trucks were used in military operations.**

Cab

The cab is an enclosed space where the driver is seated. A sleeper is a compartment attached to the cab where the driver can rest while not driving. They can range from a simple 24" (0.6 m) bunk to a 120" (3.0 m) apartment-on-wheels.

Modern cabs feature air conditioning, a good sound system, and ergonomic seats (often air suspended).

Engine

Trucks can use all sorts of engines. Small trucks such as SUVs or pickups and even light medium-duty trucks use gasoline engines. Heavier trucks use four stroke turbo diesel engines, although there are alternatives. Huge off-highway trucks use locomotive-type engines such as a V12 Detroit Diesel two stroke engine.

Parts of a truck

Seats

In general, the vehicle is equipped with one or two seats for any passenger beside the driver. In recent years, however, manufacturers have approved models capable of carrying more people, sleeps up to nine . The Italian law provides that on board the truck there can only be the driver and persons directly related to loading and unloading of cargoes; therefore, these passengers cannot be compared to those of cars.

The driver's seat of a truck must always be protected from any movement of objects carried. This is achieved by keeping separate the cab from the cargo area or applying a protective partition behind the driver in case of a single body compartment.

The classic truck is one in which the cargo space, whether it be van tarpaulin, is completely separated from the cockpit.

The truck frames are provided with a variable number of drive gear, usually 2 or 3 for the most common uses, and the engine is usually equipped with wheels. The more modern are equipped with air springs that provide the means to an optimum level   regardless of load carried and also allow a more comfortable ride.

> The Volvo FH is the most successful range of trucks Volvo has ever built. In 2000, the FH12 was awarded the 'Truck of the Year.'

11

TRUCKS

The engines currently produced are strictly diesel. The drive gear is a mechanical lever, while the gearbox is generally controlled by a button on the gear knob itself. In heavy vehicles, especially those used for towing trailers or semitrailers, the change typically consists of a box base, which is typically 3 or 4 gears plus reverse, and a range selector gear places respectively downstream and upstream of case basis.

The truck loading areas of common use are characterized by a width that easily allows you to load the goods on pallets, typically 240 cm, with a base level and made of wood or aluminium. The effective height for the load is around 280 cm in the most modern methods available to low-frame chassis and suspension. The vehicle has an average length of about 6 m, but useful, reaching the maximum permitted overall limit. There are even boxes with lengths up to 10/10, 5 m (12 ft to stay in total, about 2 m cabin + 10 m of body).

Even for the transport of dangerous goods (ADR) the approval for the cargo is subject to certain conditions.

There must be fire resistant materials for the cover that covers the outside and must indicate on the cargo marking the type of goods being transported and the nature of the hazard. Tables of the same type must be indicated on the sides and front of the car, outside the cab. In addition, vehicles carrying dangerous goods must have a specific setting which consists of shielded electrical cables and connections.

Parts of a truck

For stability and safety during the lifting of materials through the crane, which must be strictly stationary, is equipped with 4 independent outriggers, hydraulic controls, to adapt to every shape of land and prevent dangerous movements of the load being handled.

A device in a truck called a 'switch' allows you to isolate the battery from the rest of the vehicle by turning on a switch.

Presence of equipment for fire-fighting is a must and the crew of the vehicle must know the use. The fire extinguishers must meet a recognized standard and be sealed to ensure that they are not used. The date by which the next inspection should take place should also be mentioned.

The most common use is for the loading of diggers, bulldozers, forklifts etc and for deliveries of heavy materials in places where there are no loading docks and appropriate equipments (e.g. construction sites).

Maintenance of trucks

Fluid checks

Trucks use a fair amount of fluids to perform its everyday tasks. So, it is important you check the fluids regularly. Check the fluids once a month. The fluids include the brake fluid, coolant, oil and power steering fluid. It is best to check the oil once the engine has warmed up for 10 minutes. Oil expands as it cools and constricts as it heats up, so you will get the most accurate reading when the engine is warm. When you buy your truck, whether it is new or used, make sure you have an owner's manual. It will tell you what type of fluids to use and what the maintenance schedule for the truck should be.

Changing the oil is probably the best insurance you can have to keep a truck running better and longer. Schedules vary from manufacturer to manufacturer, but this does not take into consideration the extra work expected out of your truck. Opinions vary, but it is a safe bet that if you change the oil every 3 to 4 thousand kilometres and change the filter in the process, your vehicle will last much longer. Often, a delivery vehicle spends a lot of time in stop and go traffic, and will spend more time idling than a normal vehicle. For this reason, the oil breaks down quicker. Changing often and using a good grade of motor oil saves a lot of wear and tear.

Maintenance of trucks

Advanced maintenance

If driving a heavy-duty truck, grease the moving parts in the truck's engine weekly. Change the fluids and power components in your vehicle according to the hours you are driving. The oil should be changed every 250 hours of driving, while the automatic transmission fluid and the standard transmission fluid should be changed every 500 and 1000 hours, respectively. The rear differentials, a component of your trucks axle, should have its fluid changed every 600 hours; the power steering, what makes the truck turn easily even though it weighs more than a ton, should have its fluid changed every 1600 km.

Extras

Add extras to your engine to keep it running efficiently, such as fluid add-ons that aid performance. Add engine coolant to your hydraulic system to keep engine running heat low, extends the life of your engine. Add fluid called an additive to your gasoline tank, to get better gas mileage and to keep your fuel pipes clean.

Tyre and brakes

Besides the engine of the truck, the next two things that really make it run well are the tyres and the brakes. The brakes should be always functioning perfectly and accurately. The brakes not working well can put you in a very vulnerable and dangerous position.

15

TRUCKS

Tyres need to be rotated on a regular basis to insure even wear. When tyres are rotated, it gives the mechanic an opportunity to check brakes and brake lines and look for abnormal wear. Also very important to the life of your tyres is checking the air pressure on a weekly basis. Remember that tyre pressures are focused on two things— a smoother ride and better stability. When considering that you maybe carrying loads that are a great deal more than an average vehicle, you may want to think about raising the tyre pressure a bit over the manufacturer's suggestions. Remember that a tyre that is low on air pressure generates a great deal more heat. Heat is the biggest enemy of a tyre, allowing it to wear out faster. Also, decreased tyre pressure, especially when hauling a load, can cause the vehicle to be much less stable than usual. Better to check the tyre pressure on a weekly basis than to have an accident.

Check suspension components and shocks on a regular basis. Because they bear more weight, they wear quicker. Poor suspension means a rough and dangerous ride, especially when carrying a load. It isn't uncommon for a load to shift if the shocks are not up to par.

Any abnormal sounds from the truck should be checked out immediately without wasting any time.

Repair and maintenance

Ensure that at the truck maintenance, everything is checked thoroughly by a

professional mechanic. Even something as inconsequential as lights are extremely important as they go on to alert the other drivers about the presence of the truck. Lights are quite easy to break, get cracked or not be working. Ensure that they are in the best of working conditions.

Signals and mirrors

These are the other things in your truck that will ensure your driving safety. A truck needs the right aid of turning signals in order to let the other drivers know about its next step. Also, the mirrors will allow the driver to be able to see what is behind them and the kind of traffic around them. This will make them feel more in control of driving the truck.

Battery

Periodic maintenance of the truck will ensure that the battery is working perfectly so as to allow you to be able to use the fuel optimally without any wastage.

Modern trucks have a lot more features now than in previous decades. Onboard computers allow your maintenance man to keep a closer eye on what is going on with the engine, and a lot of sensors are now used to keep an eye on such things as exhaust emission and vacuum modules. Even with all this, however, it is a necessity to keep an eye on things from both a visual view and through regularly scheduled maintenance.

Advantages

The importance of the trucking industry is rising. Trucks can access remote and hilly areas where rail lines cannot be constructed. The trucking industry enables quick, easy departure of goods and accepts smaller loads than railways.

A truck is unique because it has an open cargo bed that allows easy access for carrying large or heavy materials. Construction workers often use this area of a truck to haul their supplies to and from jobs, but there are other uses outside of work as well. If a friend or family member is moving from one town to another, a truck with a sizable cargo bed maybe of great service. Beds, furniture and moving boxes will not fit in a car but can easily be transported via a truck's cargo bed. For those who buy covers for the cargo bed, this basically turns it into an extra-large trunk space.

Trucks are heavier than smaller automobiles and allow a higher point of view on the road. The field of vision may help avoid accidents in the first place, but if an accident does occur, the largeness of a truck may deter any major injury. The height of the truck also keeps the vehicle from acquiring too much damage if colliding with another automobile (the smaller the car, the greater the damage). Trucks are not invincible, however. So remember to always drive defensively on the road and always wear a seat belt.

Disadvantages

Trucks contribute to air, noise and water pollution as automobiles. Trucks may emit lower air pollution emissions than cars per pound of vehicle mass, although the absolute level per vehicle mile travelled is higher and diesel particulate matter is especially problematic for health. With respect to noise pollution, trucks emit considerably higher sound levels at all speeds compared to typical car. This contrast is particularly strong with heavy-duty trucks. There are several aspects of truck operations that contribute to the overall sound that is emitted. Continuous sounds are those from tyres rolling on the roadway, and the constant hum of their diesel engines at highway speeds. Less frequent noises, but perhaps more noticeable, are things like the repeated sharp-pitched whistle of a turbocharger on acceleration or the abrupt blare of an exhaust brake retarder when traversing a downgrade. There has been noise regulation put in place to help control where and when the use of engine braking retarders are allowed.

Concerns have been raised about the effect of trucking on the environment, particularly as part of the debate on global warming. In the period from 1990 to 2003, carbon dioxide emissions from transportation sources increased by 20 per cent, despite improvements in vehicle fuel efficiency.

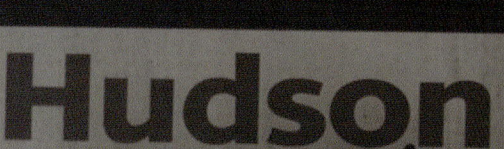

Trucking industry

Trucking firms are the link between the consumer and manufacturers. These trucking companies are contracted by businesses to pick up goods, transport them and deliver a wide variety of products that we as consumers rely on all the time. Each of these steps is carefully orchestrated so that the trucks arrive just in time to ship the goods off to their designated destinations.

The trucking industry began at the turn of the 20th century with the invention of the motorized truck. Motorized vehicles were competition for the railroad industry and became a major factor in the increase of land transportation of goods throughout the United States. The development of fuel also contributed to the increased use of trucks. As motor technology advanced and improved, there was a natural progression for the construction of paved roads. As a result, there were regulations set by the state and federal government that were to be adhered to when moving freight.

Prior to the use of trucks, trains were the most efficient mode of transporting goods because it had the capacity to accommodate bulk. Trucks were initially used to deliver items to remote locations that were inaccessible for the train. The first boom in the usage of trucks occurred during the 1920s. At this time, roads were improving which made delivery locations more accessible. Eventually more durable tyres replaced the rubber tyres and trucks were made larger in order to carry more goods while providing comfort to the driver.

Trucking industry

The first trucks were extremely heavy and had crude mechanisms. Initially, they only provided delivery and hauling to the city. This restriction was due in large part because the trucks could not handle the pothole and unpaved roads. The Automobile Club of America put on the very first United States contest for commercial vehicles; the goal of the test was to examine the reliability, speed and capacity of the truck. Excited by the results of the contest, manufacturers were to meet the demand for trucks and the use of trucks for freight transportation flourished.

The trucking industry as we know it was still in its infancy when the Great Depression hit and a number of trucking companies were forced to close their operations. The companies who survived were able to benefit from the repeal of Prohibition, which also occurred during a time of economic recovery. In 1935, Congress passed the Motor Carrier Act; this act provided structure for the industry.

The Motor Carrier Act set regulations for freight-hauling. The act limited the hours that could be driven. It also mandated the classification of freight that could be carried. The owners of the trucking companies became concerned that the new regulations would compromise their competitive advantage over established rail companies. As infrastructures were improved, driver demand increased and opened up opportunity for new businesses to enter the market.

TRUCKS

The trucking industry is a key player in an economy through the transportation of raw materials, produces and finished goods. Trucks are also vital to the construction industry when large amounts of materials are needed for a project.

Under the regulation of ICC, companies who have for-hire trucks were required to apply for a license if they wanted like to enter the interstate markets. The guidelines were strict and licenses were granted only if it could be proven that there was a need for additional capacity. The rates, which used to be an agreement between the trucker and the customer, were put in the hands of bureaus. The rate bureaus are owned and administered by participating carriers. The bureaus job is to analyze costs and initiate pricing standards and competitive rates within the industry. In 1980, Congress put through a trucking deregulation bill. The goal of the bill was to increase competition and this competition resulted in reduced shipping costs for customers.

Prior to 1983, truck size and weight limitations were set by individual states. The federal government pushed for legislation that set limitations on the interstate highway system. In addition to increasing the size and weight limitations on truck, the law also resulted in an increase of the national gas tax and increased fees on the industry. Currently, the trucking industry is responsible for paying roughly half of all state and federal road user taxes.

Famous truck manufacturers

Isuzu

Isuzu Motors Ltd. is a Japanese car, commercial vehicle and heavy truck manufacturing company, headquartered in Tokyo. In 2005, Isuzu became the world's largest manufacturer of medium to heavy duty trucks. It has assembly and manufacturing plants in the Japanese city of Fujisawa, as well as in the prefectures Tochigi and Hokkaidō. Isuzu is famous for producing commercial vehicles and diesel engines. By 2009, Isuzu had produced over 21 million diesel engines, which can be found in vehicles all over the world. Isuzu diesel engines are used by Renault, Opel and General Motors.

Volvo Trucks

Volvo is the second largest producer of heavy duty trucks in the world. There are few countries you can visit where there isn't a Volvo truck on the road.

Based in Sweden, Volvo trucks is a truck manufacturer owned by the Volvo Group. The company currently employs over 22,000 people around the world and has its global headquarters in Gothenburg.

Volvo trucks produce and sell over 100,000 trucks each year. Approximately 95 per cent of the trucks they produce are in the heavy weight class above 16 tonnes. A large proportion of Volvo trucks are manufactured in the USA along with Sweden, Brazil and Belgium.

Both Volvo Trucks and the automobiles produced by the Volvo Group are renowned for their safety record and are considered to be some of the safest vehicles in the world. They are also incredibly reliable and durable.

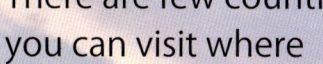

TRUCKS

Daimler AG

Daimler AG is a German car corporation. It is the thirteenth largest car manufacturer and second largest truck manufacturer in the world. In addition to automobiles, Daimler manufactures buses and provides financial services through its Daimler Financial Services arm. The company also owns major stakes in aerospace group EADS, high-technology and parent company of the Vodafone McLaren Mercedes racing team McLaren Group (which currently is in the process of becoming a fully independent stand-alone corporate entity), and Japanese truck maker Mitsubishi Fuso Truck and Bus Corporation.

Daimler produces cars and trucks under the brands of Mercedes-Benz, Maybach, Smart, Freightliner and many others.

Tata Motors

Tata Trucks are amongst the most sought-after heavy commercial vehicles (HCV) in India. Products of Tata Motors Limited – the largest automobile company in India with a consolidated revenues of Rs. 70,938,85 crores (in 2008-09), Tata Trucks not only outplayed its competitors by its qualities, but also by its services.

Tata Motors is the fourth largest truck manufacturer in the world. Established in 1945, it first rolled out its vehicle in 1954. Since then, more than 4 million Tata vehicles run on the Indian roads. It has its manufacturing units located in various locations across the country including Jamshedpur, Pantnagar, Pune, Dharwad and Lucknow.

Tata Trucks have created a niche in the truck industry worldwide. Tata Trucks also lead in the key medium and heavy truck category with an index of 90 in the segment of Tractor-Trailer.

Famous truck manufacturers

PACCAR Inc

PACCAR Inc is the third largest manufacturer of heavy-duty trucks in the world and has substantial manufacture in light and medium vehicles through its various subsidiaries.

Based in Bellevue, Washington, it was founded in 1905 by William Pigott, Sr., as the Seattle Car Manufacturing Company. Its original business was the production of railway and logging equipment. Upon a subsequent merger with a Portland, Oregon firm, Twohy Brothers, Seattle Car Manufacturing Company became the Pacific Car and Foundry Company.

Pacific Car and Foundry purchased Seattle's Kenworth Motor Truck Company in 1945 and both Peterbilt Motors Company and Dart Truck Company 13 years later. In 1972 the corporate name was officially changed to PACCAR Inc, with the Pacific Car and Foundry Company name being assigned to a division thereof.

MAN SE

MAN is one of Europe's leading manufacturers of commercial vehicles, engines and mechanical engineering equipment. The group supplies trucks, buses, diesel engines as well as turbo machinery. MAN primarily operates in Europe. It is headquartered in Munich, Germany and employs more than 47,740 people.

The MAN Group is one of Europe's leading industrial players in transport-related engineering, with revenue of approximately €14.7 billion in 2010. As a supplier of trucks, buses, diesel engines, turbo machinery and special gear units, MAN employs approximately 47,700 people worldwide. Its divisions hold leading positions in their respective markets.

TRUCKS

Some famous trucks

The Terex Titan

The Terex Titan was manufactured by General Motors of Canada. It is the world's largest tandem axle truck ever built to this date. It measures a whopping 20 m long and 6.8m tall. When its dump box is extended, it is capable of standing at 17 m tall, the equivalent of five stories!

The Terex Titan is powered by a 16 cylinder locomotive engine and delivers 3300 horsepower. The cylinder was combined with a huge generator to deliver power to 4 traction engines located on the real wheels. The generator alone has enough power to supply 250 homes with electricity.

Back in 1978, one Titan was brought to Sparwood, B.C. from California, for use in a mine. The truck was too large to be moved by road, so it arrived by train on 8 flatbed cars. It was re-assembled and driven to the mine.

The tyres are 3.5 m in diameter, and weigh 4 tons each. Two Greyhound buses and two pick-up trucks would fit inside its dumper.

The Titan is no longer used because of the huge expenditure needed to keep it running. This truck is a tourist attraction in Sparwood, British Columbia, Canada.

> The Terex Titan was first shown to the public in Las Vegas at the American Mining Congress.

Some famous trucks

The Caterpillar 797

The Caterpillar 797 mining truck was the largest of its kind in the world until 2001. Brought into operation in 2000, it has a payload capacity of 360 tons. It is powered by a 24 cylinder V24 quad-turbo diesel engine that produces an amazing 3,400 horsepower. The truck is 7 m from the road to the top of truck bed, and almost 15 m tall when the bed is raised for dumping. The total length of the truck is 14.4 m.

Eight onboard computers monitor oil pressure, transmission torque, engine performance and tyre temperature. The Caterpillar 797 sells for $3.4 million; the 3.9 m tall Michelin tyres were especially designed for the 797, and cost about $30,000 each.

With a full load, the 797 can move as fast as 64 km/h on level ground.

The truck uses fuel in huge amounts, an average of 65 gallons/hr with a fuel economy rating of 0.3 mpg. With such huge costs involved, the vehicle is usually run 24 hours per day, 365 days per year, stopping only for regularly scheduled maintenance.

The DT60 became the most popular engine in heavy duty trucks in the 1990s. This was due to its reliability and fuel economy.

TRUCKS

Liebherr T 282B

The Liebherr T 282B is a large earth-hauling dump truck designed by Liebherr, a German manufacturer of heavy equipment, household appliances, microelectronics, car parts, tool machines and aerospace components.

Launched in 2004, it became the largest earth-hauling truck in the world. The T 282B is an updated version of the T 282 truck. The trucks are assembled in a 10 acre (4 hectare) factory in Newport News, Virginia, USA, that can handle four 282s at a time.

The T 282B has an empty weight of 203 tonnes and a maximum capacity of 365 tonnes. The maximum operating weight is 592 tonnes. It is 14.5 m long and 7.4 m tall over the canopy, with a wheelbase of 6.6 m. The top speed of the truck is 65 km/h.

The truck costs about US$ 3.5 million. A CD-player and air conditioning systems are listed on the optional equipment spec, unusual in the world of professional hauling. Liebherr sells up to a few dozen of them every year, primarily to coal, copper, iron and gold mines in USA, Chile, Indonesia, South Africa and Australia.

> A salt shaker is a snow plow. Truckers call the snow plow a salt shaker because of its ability to spread salt on the highways during icy conditions on the highway.

Some famous trucks

Dekotora

Dekotora or Decotora is the local abbreviation for 'Decoration Truck'. They are sometimes known as the Art Trucks too. The truckers of Japan love to decorate their trucks with shiny stainless or golden exterior parts, beautifully painted landscapes, kabuki or manga characters or pictures of celebrities. At night, their fluorescent handiwork comes to life with colourful and bold neon and ultraviolet light displays. These decorations usually adorn the cab as well as the trailer, on the exterior as well as in the interior.

Decotora truck owners are very passionate about the looks of their decorated trucks. They have an emotional attachment with their trucks and do not care about the money they spend in decorating these trucks. What gives them the satisfaction and pride is the personalization and symbolic meaning of these art designs on their trucks. The trucks look like artsy monsters after decoration. Seeing this large scale decoration, anybody could easily confuse these Dekotora trucks to be something art related but automotive. Despite of so much decoration Dekotora trucks still retain their performance ability and are used as reliable workhorses.

Owners of these decorated Japanese trucks often form groups or Dekotora communities. They organize shows to showcase Dekotora trucks and arrange competitions for best decorated trucks.

TRUCKS

Monster Trucks

Known for its extraordinarily big wheels, the monster truck is part of a very popular sports entertainment that is closely associated with other events such as car-eating robots, tractor pulls and mud bogging. Due to the ordinarily massive design of this vehicle, many people are easily attracted to it.

Upon seeing a monster truck, it is very hard to notice its massive tyres, which go very well with its equally large body frame. This type of vehicle uses Terra tyres, each of which measures 1.7 by 1.1 by 0.6 m or 66 by 43 by 25 inches. Its engines have displacement of more or less 575 cubic inches. Aside from these things, it is also important to look at its custom-designed or modified automatic transmission, which makes use of versions like the Ford C6 transmission, the Power glide as well as the Turbo 400.

In terms of design, this kind of truck features a tubular chassis that is custom-built, supercharged engines and modified axles. Likewise, it also has four-wheel steering for better driving control. Trucks with automatic transmissions usually come with heavy-duty gear sets, manual valve bodies and transbrakes.

Although monster trucks run only in small arenas, the safety and well-being of drivers and spectators are highly important. Before drivers can participate, they need to wear head and neck restraints, helmets and safety harnesses. To prevent them from burning in case accidents arise, they are also required to use fire suits.

> The world's largest monster truck is Bigfoot 5. It weighs 17236 kg and stands a giant 15 ft 6 inches tall, sporting 10 ft tall Firestone Tundra tyres.

Test Your MEMORY

1. What are trucks?

2. Write briefly about the history of trucks.

3. Name the types of trucks.

4. What are the parts of a truck?

5. Write briefly about truck maintenance.

6. What are the advantages of a truck?

7. What are the disadvantages of a truck?

8. Write briefly about the trucking industry.

9. Name two famous truck manufacturers.

10. Write briefly about Isuzu truck manufacturers.

11. What are Dekotora trucks?

12. What are monster trucks?

Index

B

Battery 17
brake fluid 14
brakes 5, 6, 15, 16

C

cab 3, 6, 10, 11, 12, 29
Cab 10
cargo space 11
Caterpillar 797 27
CB 6
chassis 3, 6, 9, 10, 12, 30
Chassis 10
cockpit 4, 11
coolant 14, 15
crane 13

D

Daimler AG 24
Daimler-Motoren-Gesellschaft 4
Dekotora 29, 31
disc brakes 6
drive gear 11, 12

E

Engine 10

G

Garbage Trucks 8
gearbox 12

H

horsepower 4, 6, 26, 27
hydraulic system 15

I

Isuzu Motors Ltd 23

L

Liebherr T 282B 28

M

MAN SE 25
mirrors 17

O

oil 14, 15, 27

P

PACCAR Inc 25
Pickup Trucks 8
pollution 19
power steering fluid 14

R

Rigid Trucks 7

S

Signals 17
switch 13

T

Tata Motors Limited 24
Terex Titan 26
Tippers 7
Tyres 15, 16
Truck 3, 11, 24, 25, 29
trucking industry 3, 18, 20, 21, 22, 31
turbocharger 6, 19

V

vehicle 3, 4, 5, 8, 9, 11, 12, 13, 14, 15, 16, 18, 19, 23, 24, 27, 30
Volvo Trucks 23